The Amazons of South America

A MESSENGER ARMED ONLY WITH A KNIFE CONCEALED UNDER HIS CLOAK.

The Amazons of South America

Spanish Adventurers and the People of the
Great River of South America,
15th to the 19th Centuries

C. M. Stevens

LEONAUR

The Amazons of South America
Spanish Adventurers and the People of the Great River of South America,
15th to the 19th Centuries
by C. M. Stevens

First published under the title
The Amazons of South America

Leonaur is an imprint of Oakpast Ltd

Copyright in this form © 2012 Oakpast Ltd

ISBN: 978-0-85706-988-7 (hardcover)
ISBN: 978-0-85706-989-4 (softcover)

http://www.leonaur.com

Contents

South American Amazons

Women have borne such heroic parts in the battles of tribes and nations that no surprise or sentiment was felt when reports came from Manila that many, clothed as men, were found among the insurgent dead. History, both fabulous and authentic, abounds in martial deeds of the so-called non-combatants. But from no source has there come such wild stories as from the early explorers of South America.

In the sixteenth century the belief was universal that there were tribes in America domineered wholly by women. Columbus, in one of his reports, wrote a full account of an island inhabited entirely by women, and Cortes, in a letter to the Emperor Charles V, gives a description of a province peopled only by amazons. De Soto and Sir Walter Raleigh left testimony of their existence, and almost every explorer, missionary, conqueror and historian from Columbus to Condamine and Humboldt, believed in the stories of women warriors. Like all such accounts, error was mixed with truth, and the error so predominated that the stories of the amazons have been by general consent relegated to the shades of myth and fiction. However, there were tribes of South American amazons, not from choice, but by accident and necessity. The adventures of the early sea rovers and explorers amply attest this fact.

One of the most curious incidents is related of a crew from the French buccaneering fleet of Le Sieur Maubenon. Off the coast of Venezuela in 1674, one of the vessels was separated from the others in a storm and driven among the dangerous reefs of Los Roques. Desperate efforts were made to save the ship, but it struck on a rock, and the crew had barely time to get into the long boat, without an ounce of water or food, before the ship went down. They were driven helplessly until nearly midnight, when they were cast upon a low, marshy shore. Making the best of their situation, they waited until morning, hoping they were upon the mainland, where they might have reasonable expectation of escape. At the first appearance of daylight they ascended a neighbouring hill, and discovered they were on a small island, in the centre of which was an Indian village of unusual size.

As but one gun and half a dozen swords had been saved, it was necessary to be very cautious; but their hunger was so pressing that little delay was made in making their presence known. Fortifying themselves as securely as possible on the side of the hill nearest their boat, they sent a messenger, armed only with a knife concealed under his cloak, to test the friendliness of the natives. So far they had seen only women and children about the huts, but a huge circular house, surrounded by a rude palisade, obstructed part of the view.

An unusual commotion was visible in the village as the peace messenger approached, and the inhabitants disappeared. This puzzled the courier as much as it did his comrades, for he spent an interminable time in reconnoitring. As he approached nearer, half a dozen well-aimed arrows admonished him not to approach within range of the palisades around the big circular house. The Frenchmen knew that their comrade, Pierre Lescat, was brave enough for any adventure, but it was very disquieting to see him disappear among the huts. The buccaneers waited until they became convinced that something ill had befallen him, when they set out to accomplish his rescue. Half way to the village they saw a column of smoke rising from the centre of the circular house, as if for a signal, and soon after Lescat appeared, carrying enough cassava cakes and nuts to make them a welcome breakfast. The information he brought was most astonishing.

The island was inhabited only by women, and was the famous home of the amazons. Their reputation for implacable fierceness was also well sustained, for no one dared within arrow-shot of the palisade. Efforts were continued throughout the day to open friendly communication with them, since no more food was to be found, with the result that two of the more venturesome were severely wounded. That night, in place of the column of smoke, a bonfire was kept burning, and sentinels armed with bows and spears could be seen guarding every part of the palisades. When morning came the buccaneers made a thorough search for food, but could find none. After another effort to open negotiations, the pangs of hunger made them determine to capture the storehouse and stronghold by assault. A number of long poles were procured, and a rush was made from behind the nearest cabin against the palisades. A wide strip of the defences was torn down, but the assailants were obliged to drop their poles and run, with numerous severe wounds from the well-directed shafts of the defenders.

Pierre Lescat then conceived a brilliant plan for destroying the defences. Three or four movable blockhouses were made of the thatched roofs from the huts, and inclosed in these the men, with their swords tied on the ends of long cane stalks, pushed their way into the enclosure, tore a wide opening through the side of the circular building, and spread their protecting screens around a huge pile of cassava bread, nuts, and bucanned meat. The feasting that followed was not altogether pleasant, since the women were ranged around the wall and were able to send several arrows through openings in the screen. Another attempt to parley with the implacable females ended disastrously, since the moment the venturesome spokesman showed himself, an arrow tore a vicious wound in his pacifically raised arm.

The portable fortification was then moved forward and the amazons, unable to defend themselves against it, rushed outside, abandoning the storehouse to the victors. The generous instincts of the Frenchmen toward feminine distress suggested a scheme for friendly parley. Each man took an armful from the pile of provisions and followed the women, who, to the number of about a hundred, were guarding the flight of an equal number that had gone ahead with the children. In vain, with all the conciliating gestures at their command, they offered to share their captured provisions with the vanquished, but were compelled to keep out of range from the threatening arrows. An hour or more passed in these futile efforts, and the far end of the island was nearly reached, when the buccaneers, looking back from the top of a hill, saw the whole village in a mass of flames.

In great alarm they ceased their blandishments to the unappreciative females and ran breathlessly back to the burning huts. When they arrived there, nothing remained but heaps of ashes and embers. As the provisions were of the most importance, immediate search was made among the ruins of the circular house, but nothing could be found except a few baked nuts. The mystery was solved soon after, when they decided to go to the mainland, which could be seen about a league distant. To their consternation, they discovered their boat was gone. The tracks of twenty or thirty amazons and several bits of provisions found in the sand, disclosed what had occurred. A hasty consultation decided the angry Frenchmen they were no longer bound to respect the sex of these cannibal Caribs.

Depositing in a place of safety the precious provisions which they had offered to the ungrateful females as an earnest of pacific intentions, the buccaneers marched back to the far end of the island with the stern determination to recapture their boat at any cost, but when they arrived there nothing was to be seen but a score of canoes about a mile from land, heading for an adjacent island. Curses availed nothing, and they returned to spend the night at the place where they had left their scanty provisions.

When morning came a new danger menaced them, for, during the night, two or three hundred warriors had landed near them. Doubtless these were the men of the village, who had returned from hunting or fighting. The buccaneers fortified themselves and prepared to withstand the attack, which soon came. Their chief hope lay with Pierre Lescat and his musket. With this he was able to keep the Indians away during the day, but by nightfall he had fired his last charge and the next day they expected to fall before the overwhelming numbers of the savages. Just before daybreak they were beside themselves with joy at hearing the boom of a cannon. A ship from Le Sieur Maubenon's fleet had been sent out to search for them, and it had arrived in the niche of time. The savages fled and the Frenchmen spread their story among the buccaneers. Many a wild yarn of the sea-rovers is directly traceable to the amazons of Los Roques.

The Spanish annals are especially full of romantic encounters with amazons. Condamine in 1743 found a chief who claimed to have been born of an Amazon mother, and this chief's son said that he had often visited the female fighters with his father, at their fortified town on an island in the Rio Negro. Orellana and his Dominican followers in Brazil made many attempts to carry the gospel to these benighted women, but were never permitted to enter their territory. In descending the Amazon River, then known as the Maranon, he was warned by many *caciques* not to attempt to pass a certain settlement, as it was possessed by a tribe of women so fierce that none ever survived who entered their territory unbidden. Even the phenomenally savage band of Lope de Aguirre turned aside from their course in 1560, fearing to pass through the lands of these fierce warrior women.

Early in 1541, Orellana had a battle with a savage tribe at the mouth of the Frombretas River. He says that with them was a band of amazons who fought with greater fierceness than he had ever seen. They used bows and stone hatchets, while some bore shields and spears. They were unconquerable and did not desist from, killing as long as they could draw breath. He described them as "tall, robust and fair, with long hair twisted over their heads, and with undressed skins around their loins." So great was their fame that the Spanish Government sent out several expeditions to conquer them and every explorer was charged with the duty to take special note of any information concerning them, so that they might be brought to a knowledge of the Cross. But the strange tribe of savage females were always just beyond the farthest point which the explorer had been able to reach. D'Acuna made a systematic investigation through Brazil in 1639, and from a sceptic became a firm believer in the existence of these untamable creatures. He claimed to have found irrefutable proof that they were located at that time on the River Cunuriz.

In consequence. Count Pagan, through the friendly offices of a neighbouring chief, was allowed to have a conference with a deputation of amazons. Great interest and sympathy was aroused for them in Christendom, and they became the objects of unbounded solicitude among the Ecclesiastics. Several histories were written of them, and one by L'Abbe Gujon claimed that the most sacred and glorious task ever appearing before the Church was the conversion of these deluded women. Father Cyprian Baraza, a Jesuit missionary, wrote a sensational letter to his superiors in Spain, giving a remarkable story of a visit to them in 1690. They allowed him to preach to them through his interpreters for three successive days and then ordered him to leave the country, saying that they once had a god, but he had abandoned them, and they would have no other. They were then just west of the Paraguay, at the twelfth degree south latitude.

Several years later, another Jesuit missionary, Father Gili, wrote that he had visited a tribe of amazons on the Chuchivera River near where it empties into the Orinoco, and met with a similar experience from the unteachable barbarians. Even as late as 1848, the natives unanimously declared that hordes of female warriors ruled with dreadful barbarity the whole territory of the upper Corentyn in the Marawonne country, and the Macusi Indians showed immense heaps of broken pottery at numerous places in the forests as proofs of former dwelling places of the amazons, they being the only persons ever in that region who had a taste for such ornaments.

One of the best authenticated stories of the amazons is recorded by Hernando de Ribeira, a follower of Cabeza de Vega. In 1543 he went on an expedition far up a branch of the Paraguay River into the lands of the Urtuezez Indians. The *caciques* everywhere told him that about ten days' journey to the northwest would bring him into a territory whose inhabitants were composed wholly of women. They were said to be in no way offensive or aggressive, but no man had been known to enter their domains uninvited and come out alive. For the first time, a natural origin was ascribed to their anomalous government. It was said that they had been a powerful tribe, living as other tribes, but at war with all their neighbours.

One of their most aggressive enemies, in a sudden raid, burnt the principal village and slew the chief with his entire family. His warriors swore that they would destroy the offending tribe or be destroyed themselves. The women and children were all placed in the chief remaining village, and it chanced to be that every male was capable of accompanying the expedition, and all were pressed into service. The enemy, hearing of the approaching warriors, formed a coalition of tribes, set a powerful ambush, and, surrounding the coming enemy, succeeded in killing them all. The victors determined to extirpate the tribe, but the women built palisades, barricaded their houses, and fought so desperately that the enemy was obliged to retire without having accomplished their object. From that time on the women had successfully defended their homes from all encroachments, had slain all their male offspring as useless appendages, and had allowed no man to enter their territory except upon invitation.

The seat of their government was on an island in a lake known as the Mansion of the Sun, because of the golden ornaments that covered the houses of the Amazon rulers, and which were reflected so brilliantly in the still water. The *caciques* of the Urtuezez nation were unanimous in their testimony that the amazons had such an abundance of white and yellow metal taken from their own mines that all their utensils and weapons were made therefrom. No greater lure could come in the way of the Spaniards, and a messenger was sent at once to entreat permission for the white strangers to come and teach them the true religion of the Cross. To the sorrow of Ribeira, the answer was returned that only three of the Christian priests with their interpreter, would be allowed to come, and that under the penalty of death they must come unarmed, obey the laws, and remain no longer than three days.

As it happened, Father Aldeno was the only priest with the expedition, but two others readily volunteered to assume the office and face the danger. A month after the three men set out on their strange mission, Ribeira was compelled to return to the nearest reduction or missionary post on the Paraguay, without any tidings of the absent men.

The Urtuezez chiefs gravely advanced the opinion that the Spaniards had in some way violated the laws of the country and had suffered the penalty. They offered to find out what had happened, rescue the men if possible, and, in any event, to report the matter to Ribeira at an early date. It was several hundred miles to the Spanish reduction, and several weeks must elapse before the fate of the visitors to the amazons could be known, but the Indians promised all possible haste.

Six months later, the interpreter, who had gone with the three Spaniards, appeared at the reduction with a remarkable story of his escape. He brought the first information that the Urtuezez chiefs could obtain of the fate of the Spaniards. He said that Father Aldeno had performed his duties faithfully and won the respect of the women chiefs, but that the two bogus priests had from the first neglected their duties and had busied themselves offensively with the golden ornaments and in flattering the vanity of the younger women. Father Aldeno and the interpreter had warned them in vain. Suitable presents were exchanged, and they set out on their return. The third night after their departure, the priest and the interpreter were struck with consternation to find that the two Spaniards had succeeded in enticing two of the younger amazons to follow them.

They had evidently stolen away, with all the gold they could carry, on the night following the departure of the visitors, and succeeded in overtaking their lovers on the third night. Nothing remained but to get as far from pursuit as possible. As the Spaniards refused to part with their prizes, they broke camp at once and the homeward journey became a flight. The interpreter had warned them that the neighboring tribes were friendly to the amazons, and that all villages must be avoided. However, the next day they suddenly came upon a camp of Indian hunters, who at once surrounded them and inquired how the two amazon girls came to be with them. Excuses were of no avail. Bribes and threats likewise effected nothing. According to their treaty with the amazons, they were obliged to return all runaways and their seducers. This could be no exception. Their hands were bound and a dozen warriors were deputed to take the prisoners back to the Mansion of the Sun.

Hardly had they begun the return march, when they were met by a score of amazons in hot pursuit. The fugitives were turned over to the warrior women, who took them back to the outraged community for trial and punishment. As a result the interpreter and the priest were sold as slaves to a fierce tribe half a month's journey to

SIX MONTHS LATER, THE INTERPRETER APPEARED AT THE REDUC-
TION WITH A REMARKABLE STORY OF HIS ESCAPE.

the north, while the two Spaniards and their *inamoratas* were placed together in a singular prison which the amazons had constructed for such malefactors. The Indian interpreter, after a time, succeeded in making his escape, but the priest bowed to his hard servitude as being the will of God. According to the best that the interpreter could learn, the prison made for the malefactors of the amazons, consisted of a high circular wall around a small island in the lake. In this place were thrown all who disobeyed the laws, where they were kept without clothing or shelter during the remainder of their miserable existence. Their sole subsistence was derived from whatever they could grow in the soil, and from the food to be procured in exchange for the ornaments they could make from the clay and stone found in the earth of the enclosure.

Such was the horror inspired by this place, that the laws were implicitly obeyed, and there had never been more than a dozen persons at one time thus imprisoned. The Spaniards at the Jesuit reductions were eager to conquer the amazons and release their comrades, but they were too few in number for such an enterprise and the project was abandoned. It was fifty years before white men again penetrated the region. This was done by the Portuguese from Brazil. They found the territory about the Mansion of the Sun occupied by a flourishing tribe, who had many stories and traditions concerning the subjugation of the amazons by a neighbouring tribe, but there was nothing to establish the unquestionable identity of the race of women warriors.

Some historians suppose that the habit of the Guarani-Brazilian race of Indians of wearing combs in their long hair, which was usually knotted upon their heads feminine fashion, gave rise to the many extraordinary stories about the amazons. It is certain that in the territory of these Indians, the most persistent reports of female tribes were met with.

For two hundred years there was a universal belief that a nation of women ruled over a vast area of South America. The Portuguese and Spaniards were continually producing individuals who had escaped from these strange women after experiencing adventures which would be incredible to any but such mystery-loving people. The Dutch and French were but little behind their neighbours in wonderful stories of these remarkable women. The English alone, however credulous, seem never to have found any evidence worthy of record. Southey, the painstaking English historian of Brazil, summed up all the evidence very carefully and came to the conclusion that there were no tribes of amazons.

In the stories recorded by the French explorers, that of Jean Villiers awakened the greatest interest. He had been lost on one of their expeditions on the Orinoco, and after three or four years appeared at the settlements in Guiana, claiming that he had been captured by a tribe of amazons. According to his story, they had cultivated and refined their minds, while the men were degraded and brutalized by continual war, till they became greatly superior, and, for that reason, refused to live subject to the inferior habits of the men. The female children they bore were of their own exalted instincts and tastes, but their male offspring were invariably of the brutish and inferior type of their fathers. Therefore the women had gone into a community by themselves, refusing to associate with their husbands except as the fancy pleased them. He said that they were so fond of gold and silver ornaments, and those metals were so little esteemed among the other Indian tribes, that they had succeeded in collecting nearly all the gold and silver in the country, with which they adorned their persons and houses.

To this cause he attributed the dearth of precious metals in the French territories. In support of the truth of his story, he loaded two pack mules with trinkets dear to feminine eyes, and disappeared in the forests for three months or more. On his return he showed a rich exchange of curiously wrought gold and silver ornaments. In subsequent visits to the amazons, he refused all partnerships in his enterprise, and nothing could induce him to reveal the source of his rapidly growing wealth. The romantic stories he told concerning his experience among the wonderful tribe of females were the sensation of his time, but he successfully defeated all efforts made to ferret out his peculiar patronesses, and returned to France with his secret and his wealth.

Portales, the Spanish Governor of Venezuela, was so aroused by the stories of Villiers, that he sent out a searching party, which was gone nearly a year. They reported that the so-called amazons of Villiers were a kind of religious order of women, who lived on an island in the Rio Negro, after the manner of the virgins of the sun. There were less than a hundred of them, and their gold came from the surrounding tribes as a religious offering or tribute. As the Spaniards came back empty-handed, with the loss of three-fourths of their number through the hardships they had undergone, it was strongly suspected that their story was made as an excuse for the failure of their expedition.

Francisco Torralva, in behalf of the Spanish Government, made a very extended search and his report located an extensive tribe of amazons in western Guiana, whom he invested with all the romance of the day. But, regardless of the overwhelming testimony of both priests and adventurers, their identity was never sufficiently established to satisfy modem belief.

Many ingenious theories have been advanced to explain the incredible stories that were so implicitly believed for more than two centuries, as well as to account for the actual existence of the amazons, but the true origin of the persistent and prevailing testimony will doubtless remain a mystery.

The Peruvian accounts of the amazons are all incidental to the search for the golden riches of El Dorado. Perhaps none are so well attested as those recorded among the adventures of the followers of the younger Almagro. After the decisive Battle of Chupas, a considerable band of the defeated "men of Chili" escaped across the Andes to the unknown regions east of Cuzco. They descended into the tropical forests of Caravaya, and there broke up into small parties, some of which took Indian wives and founded towns. Among these were Sandia, San Gobin, and San Juan del Oro. So much gold was sent to Spain from Del Oro, that Charles V gave it the title of Royal City. Eventually the Chunche Indians of the Sirineyri tribe massacred all the Spaniards east of the Andes and burnt their towns. Until as late as 1852, no attempt was made to penetrate these regions, except by the Peruvian bark-hunters. Curious evidences of Spanish civilization are still to be found in the overgrown ruins of these forest cities.

The Cascarilleros, as the bark-hunters were called, often brought the most romantic stories of Spanish-Indian tribes, living aloof from the natives, with strange barbaric splendour in the midst of the almost impenetrable forests. These stories were readily believed, since about this time, an extensive tribe, known as the Jeberos, was found on the Amazon by the Dominican missionaries, every member of which received the homage of the surrounding tribes from being the offspring of Spanish women captured in the insurrections of 1599. One of these tribes of the Caravaya forests, living in almost religious seclusion, claimed to be descendants of the "children of the sun" and an exalted band of noble amazons. Some representatives of the tribe crossed the Andes with the Cascarilleros and visited the Spanish settlements. There could be no question of their Spanish descent, but they refused to allow a priest to return with them and warned the Spaniards not to visit them.

The discovery of this tribe gave colour to one of the marvellous stories that had long been related among the adventures of the "men of Chili" who had escaped across the Andes from the rage of Vaca de Castro.

This remnant of the veteran soldiery of Almagro found so little opposition in the great tropical forests beyond the mountains that they divided into congenial bands and sought their fortunes separately. One of these, consisting of Spanish knights, became lost and wandered for an unknown time through the flowery jungles. At last they came to a most singular obstruction. It consisted of a row of cedar trees with thickly growing shrubs so intertwined with vines as to be impenetrable. At one place they hewed an opening with their swords to the distance of ten feet without relief. Then they followed the green wall until it came to an abrupt turn, as if the strange forest were of rectangular form. Following on to the distance of nearly a league, they came to a clear, cold stream flowing through the wall; and, as it was growing dark, they decided to camp there for the night.

As darkness came on they were amazed to hear the melancholy chant of many feminine voices accompanied by the tinkle of castanets and the soft tones of some reed instrument like a flute. Nothing could exceed the interest with which they waited the coming day. With the first break of dawn, the score of adventurers, who were veterans in wonders as well as in war, refreshed themselves with their scanty food and set forth to penetrate the mystery before them.

Just beyond the stream, the extraordinary wall crossed a small hill, on the top of which it turned again at right angles. Here, hidden under a mass of flowering vines, they found a narrow entrance, through which they eagerly passed, but, to their amazement, after moving through the close leafy aisles for half an hour, they found themselves emerging one by one, on the outside a few steps beyond the corner where they had entered. However, in looking over their numbers, it was found that their leader, Diego de Bonilla, was missing. They waited some time, but as he did not appear, they decided to traverse the labyrinth again. To their chagrin they once more found themselves outside the wall. Nothing had been seen of the knightly cavalier under whom most of them had served since the days when they had shared in the spoils of the Inca.

While they were considering what to do, they were electrified by the appearance at the entrance of a comely Indian girl, daintily enrobed in a scarlet fabric of llama's wool. She beckoned them to follow her, and after a few steps they found themselves in a great orchard of native fruits, extending each way around the walls. A few hundred paces more brought them to a little village consisting of a score of huts, in the centre of which there was an immense arbour or bower. In this they found their leader seated on the floor, in the midst of a hundred Indian women. Diego de Bonilla knew the language of the Incas, and one of the girls was able to talk with him. During the conference, three old women, the only ones to be seen, were performing some kind of a religious ceremony.

It was soon learned that these women were the daughters of the chief men of the surrounding tribes, brought here as a sacred place of safety to escape the capture and massacre incident to their constant wars. In the season, which was just past, their fathers came with such husbands as had been selected for them, and the ones thus given in marriage were taken away, while others who had arrived within three seasons of a marriageable age, were brought there to remain until their fathers had found suitable husbands. For a month after the departure of the lucky ones with their husbands, the evenings were spent in lamentations and melancholy religious exercises. Only a few days before, in the midst of the chant bewailing their disappointment, the three old women burst in upon them with the prophecy that the gods were sending them husbands of the noblest race in the world. The prophecies of the old women were not in good repute and they were not believed, but now it was seen that they had indeed been spoken to by the gods.

The lost and wretched Spaniards were not loath to accept the gracious invitation, especially since their eager eyes had not only devoured the beauty of the prospective wives, but had observed that there were golden ornaments in such abundance as had been seen nowhere by them since the day of spoils at Caxamalca and Cuzco.

What afterward befell this paradise is not known, since Diego de Bonilla, when he deserted the colony and went back to Spain with seven llama loads of gold, discreetly remained silent on the subsequent history. He boasted a great deal of how he had drilled the women to throw the lance and help the new husbands to beat off the angry fathers of the adjoining tribes. It became the belief in Spain that this capture of the paradise was the cause of the confederation of natives which succeeded in the final destruction of all the Spaniards east of the Andes. It was also believed that Diego de Bonilla came to Spain on a special mission from his comrades, but basely deserted them with

SHE BECKONED THEM TO FOLLOW HER.

all the gold.

The Cascarilleros, or Peruvian bark-hunters, continued through several years to describe in glowing terms their contact with this strange Spanish-Indian tribe, and it is said that a great heap of ruins is still pointed out as the paradise of the amazons.

Merida, Resurrection of a Sensation in History

Americans, having invested extensively in Spanish territory, are becoming more and more interested in the resources of the vast lands to the south. Commerce may find there an inviting field, but to none can it be more captivating than to the lover of romance. If there is anything in which the Spaniard has always excelled, it is in finding material for the most romantic fiction and then living it out in his career. If a number of men were shipwrecked on a desert island, they would proceed at once to divide into factions and then to conduct themselves, as long as they lived, in a manner that would make a popular melodrama for the American stage. But the common adventurers were not alone the romance-makers of the New World. Every great discoverer, explorer and conqueror, was involved in some way with dramatic incidents and episodes more worthy of the novelist than the historian.

Even the first great navigator was not exempt. In the voluminous records concerning him, many of which have never been published, there are vague references to stories that would make highly interesting reading. One of the best of these has, for many generations, been a household legend among the peasants of Moorish Spain, but it is now fast being lost under the flow of modern interests. A stranger would doubtless be unable to glean enough of the details to get a clear understanding of the marvellous devotion that led to such a tragic career and fate as that of Merida. Her story, as gathered from scattered and indefinite sources, is without a parallel in history. We are assured that it would have made one of the most remarkable pages in the history of Columbus, if it had not been suppressed by the order of Father Perez of La Rabida and the reverend Bishop Bobadilla of the cathedral of

Seville, in the fear that a scandal might arise which would cast reflections upon the Church. Such were the extraordinary means used to promote the discovery of the New World and such was the remarkable origin of one of the world's unknown heroines. If the story is true, we are led to ask, was the discovery of America by Columbus in 1492 due to an ecclesiastical trick, or were the sovereigns of Spain influenced by divine inspiration through the strange medium of a Moorish Christian girl?

Late in the autumn of 1491, a princely retinue filed out of the little seaport of Palos de Moguer in Andalusia, on the way to take part in the glorious ceremonies in preparation for the impending fall of Granada. At the convent of Franciscan friars, dedicated to Santa Maria de Rabida, the riders stopped and asked for a drink of water from the clear, cold well of the convent. Soon after their arrival, the prior, Juan Perez, came out with a distinguished looking stranger not habited as the friars. One of the horsemen, Martin Alonzo Pinzon, sprang to the ground, and advanced to greet them with cordial deference. After a few words, the three men went to the shade of a tree nearby, where Doña Beatriz de Bobadilla, Marchioness of Moya, sat on a rude bench awaiting them. A short but earnest conference ensued, after which the three men moved away. Doña Beatriz was thus left alone for a moment, when a young girl in peasant dress, taking advantage of the opportunity, stepped from behind the great pine tree and fell on her knees before the favourite companion of Queen Isabella.

"Noble lady, do not be frightened at my strange conduct," she whispered, in great agitation. "I have visions, visions of a mission I must perform for the glory of God and the Holy Church. Take me with you to the queen and let me tell her that if she will obey the holy voice that speaks to me, her name will be imperishable in honour, countless times more glorious than for her great victory over the Moors."

At this moment Friar Perez approached, and, laying his hand upon her head, said: "Merida, my child, you here with your visions again?"

She arose with the conscious dignity of one with a divine mission and replied fervently, "Father, my voice has brought me here and I cannot leave until a way is made for me to tell my story to the queen!"

Meanwhile, the *marchioness* surveyed her singular supplicant with searching interest. The physical perfection of the Moorish Andalusian pleased her, and the simple garb of the peasant rather enhanced the religious fervour that glowed in the young messenger's earnest face. Most of the cavalcade were remounting their horses, when the learned physician, Garcia Fernandez, approached arm in arm with the great stranger, whose eyes were downcast and despondent. The peasant girl was standing with her back to the men, but she turned at the sound of their steps and looked with glowing admiration into the inspiring countenance of the one to whom the others were giving such marked attention.

With a courtesy she took a step toward him and spoke in a tone so resonant with reverent feeling that with her first words the entire company and a score or more of the Franciscan friars gathered around as curious listeners.

Christoval Colon, as an humble medium of heaven I am inspired to tell you not to despair before the dawn of the glorious achievements just before you. I see you traversing an ocean wide and long as a thousand years, toward the broken cross of a mighty continent, on which there are countless millions living in universal darkness. A new Canaan, wide and long as the ocean, you will give to the conquering sons of Spain, and the holy men of this and other Christian lands, will add another world to the glory of God. In a few weeks the fate of the Moors will be sealed and the victors will be more easily turned from the glories of war to the greater glories of the heavenly kingdom. But first another royal hearing must be secured, and I can carry such conviction to our gracious queen that she will make sure our glorious cause.

An impatient signal from the leader of the gayly caparisoned train was sounded, a hurried conference took place, and it was then decided to send Sebastian Rodriguez, the shrewd pilot of Lepe, to Santa Fe with a letter from the learned prior addressed to the spiritual emotions of the devoted queen, strongly urging another interview for a more comprehensive consideration of the great evangelical crusade proposed by Christoval Colon.

Meantime, the *marchioness* spoke a few words to Merida, and kindly dismissed her, when the great discoverer took the peasant girl's hands in his and kissed them. In a few minutes the cavalcade swept away, and Merida, with bowed head, walked down the hill and across the fields toward her cottage home.

Within the week Sebastian Rodriguez started on his mission and

A YOUNG GIRL IN PEASANT DRESS . . . FELL ON HER KNEES BEFORE THE
FAVORITE COMPANION OF QUEEN ISABELLA.

fourteen days later returned with a letter from Queen Isabella requesting Prior Perez to come at once to the court. The enthusiastic friar did not wait for the coming day, but saddled his mule and set out for Santa Fe at midnight. He rode on through the newly conquered territory of the Moors, and, arriving at Santa Fe, soon gained an opportunity to plead the cause of Columbus. As a result it was but a few days until a sum equivalent to two hundred and sixteen dollars was in the hands of the physician, Garcia Fernandez, to be expended in procuring for the prescient navigator suitable clothing in which to appear respectfully at court and pay his expenses on the way.

It was in January of 1492 when Columbus reached Santa Fe. Granada had fallen, and an eight hundred years' struggle between the Cross and the Crescent was ended with the triumph of the Cross. Vast crowds of people, wild with religious and patriotic emotion, thronged the streets and public places at all times of the day and night. Fawning courtiers and importuning applicants occupied the time of the sovereigns, and the sublime dreams of Columbus were compelled to wait for the petty ambitions of court favourites. In the midst of this magnificent vanity and pomp, he had the friendly encouragement of Father Perez and Doña Beatriz of Moya, but his spirits sank with the seemingly interminable delay. Several times he had withdrawn from the boisterous crowds and sat down in obscure places to ponder undisturbed over his fortunes and his plans. In nearly every instance, in the midst of his reveries, he had heard a voice clear and pure, like none he had ever heard except that of the peasant girl at La Rabida, saying always the same words, "Fear not, fail not. Your monitor abides."

That some encouraging friend was following him in accordance with the peculiar superstition and religious spirit of the age, did not disturb him or awaken his curiosity. However, he heeded certain warnings and recognized timely advice from the mysterious voice.

When Fernando de Talavera was made archbishop of Granada, a note was slipped into the hands of Columbus, advising him that the learned prelate would soon open negotiations for Columbus to lead the proposed expedition, but would attempt to have him be a mere subordinate with but little share in any booty or glory. The warning read:

> Know this and yield not, that the grandeur and glory of your
> coming gift to the Church and the world must not be dimmed
> by the leader being less than high admiral and viceroy over all

lands and people within the sphere of discovery.

The princely courtiers and proud church dignitaries were shocked and indignant that a penniless supplicant should ask for such a position of distinction and dignity, much less to remain immovable in the demand. After exhausting all their resources of persuasion and indignation, a final meeting was arranged for between Columbus and the royal councillors. Doña Beatriz, Marchioness of Moya, brought her strongest influence to bear to have them accept the proffered terms, but the archbishop Fernando de Talavera easily won the councillors by showing the injustice of lavishing such distinguished honours upon an impoverished, dreaming speculator of foreign birth, who would more likely bring only ridicule to the court of Spain for such gross credulity. The meeting came to naught; and, notwithstanding the encouraging assurances that were spoken to him by the unseen monitor, Columbus mounted his mule and set out for Cordova on his way to the court of France.

Meantime, a more consequential meeting took place in the private audience room of the Queen of Castile. The beautiful and sagacious Marchioness of Moya had hastily summoned to Santa Fe the ardent friend of the great enterprise, Luis de St. Angel, who was receiver of the ecclesiastical funds of Arragon. A conference was held in her private parlour. Only those who had most influence with the sovereigns of Arragon and Castile were present. With Columbus on his way to France and the immediate advisers of the king and queen all hostile, the case seemed hopeless to the little council of friends. The Marchioness of Moya opened the door of an adjoining room and presented a stranger to the despairing conference.

"Do not be astonished," she said, seating her charge before them, "at the presence of this simple peasant girl in the garb of her rude home. The Almighty Ruler employs many inscrutable ways through which to bring about voluntary obedience to His will, and not the least of them is the inspiration and presence of this girl of Palos de Moguer. Let her speak for herself."

Without further adjuration, the peasant girl began to pour forth such a fervent and eloquent stream of brilliant visions concerning the creatures of God and the lands of the world beyond the seas, that the little assembly of learned men and women were breathless and speechless with mingled emotions of superstition and religious rapture.

It has been hinted that this Moorish peasant girl of Palos was not the inspired medium of the saints, but rather the trained instrument of the Palos physician, Garcia Fernandez, taken in charge by the Marchioness of Moya to use as a religious influence, more powerful than argument, upon the emotional councillors and rulers. It has been irreverently suggested that this fact was told to her confessor at the time of her tragic death, thus keeping the name of the peasant girl Merida from the records, robbing the world of a heroine, and keeping her name from the calendar of the saints.

Nevertheless, at the end of Merida's story, the listeners were ablaze with zeal for the spread of the Church and the glory of Spain beyond the sea.

Luis de St. Angel sought immediate audience with the Queen of Castile. He was accompanied by the learned Alonzo de Quintanilla, and was at once ushered into the presence of Isabella. Then ensued one of the most passionate harangues that ever fell from the lips of a man aroused to frenzy for the exaltation and glory of his country and church. He warned, reproached, and entreated; he argued vehemently from scripture and science, and then in solemn adjuration advised her that an undoubted voice had come direct from God. The Marchioness of Moya was at hand with the inspired Merida, and the queen with glowing eagerness heard the rapturous story of the visions that foretold surpassing glory for Spain. She at once sent for the king and laid before him the new evidence. But he listened coldly. How could he engage in such a doubtful enterprise when his treasury was exhausted with his long Moorish war?

There was a moment of profound suspense, when the immortal exclamation broke forth:

I undertake the enterprise for my own crown of Castile, and I will pledge my jewels to raise the necessary funds.

St. Angel, in exultant joy, immediately dispatched a messenger to overtake the departing navigator. About six miles from Granada, the courier came upon the lonely traveller crossing the bridge of Pinos at the foot of Mount Elvira. It was with great difficulty that the doubting man could be made to believe that his eighteen weary years of waiting and pleading at the courts of kings was now at an end. But such a message from St. Angel and Doña Beatriz was not to be ignored and he turned his mule's head once more toward the kingly court at Santa Fe.

An agreement was soon effected and St. Angel advanced the necessary funds from the ecclesiastical coffers of Arragon. A few years later, in return for this loan, some of the first gold brought from the New World by Columbus was used to gild the walls of the royal saloon in the Saragoza palace, formerly the *Aljaferia* of the Moorish kings.

A distressing period of preparation ensued. Sailors could not be found who were willing to face the terrors of unknown seas against all the superstitions of the age. The scientific men furnished ridicule with which the demagogues made those sailors who were willing to go appear as a laughing stock to all their friends, while ecclesiastics inveighed against the enterprise as sacrilegious, until even the coercive measures resorted to by the king failed to secure or hold men in the service of the visionary foreigner. Then the wealthy and influential Pinzons of Palos came forward and offered to furnish one completely equipped vessel. This was accepted and the king ordered the seizure of such other vessels, crews and equipments as would complete the armament. All the world knows of the great voyage that followed, but only the peasants of Andalusia have retained in their household stories the legend that it was Merida who influenced the Pinzons to their decisive step through the miraculous visions which she revealed to them.

Among the crews there were many who had shipped as sailors merely in reckless bravado, against the raillery and bantering jests of friends. These were mostly beardless youths of the lower aristocracy, whose adventurous spirits lived chiefly on excitement. In the anxious days early in October, when the sight of land was momentarily expected, these irresponsible and mercurial novices of the sea were the ones to be thrown into the greatest raptures at the cry of land, and were the most ungovernable and rebellious at every disappointment.

On board the *Santa Maria* there was an obscure, common sailor, known as Juan Marido, who attained considerable influence over his comrades because of the unwavering serenity of his faith and his timely, fitting counsel. Often a word from him quieted the fears of the superstitious, and a look of the unobtrusive youth made the turbulent less violent in their unreasoning passions.

The mysterious voice that had cheered the great admiral at Santa Fe when he was pleading his cause at the royal court, was still with him through the perilous hours just before the dawn of his mighty triumph. Through innumerable ways, someone, unknown, kept him fully informed of every word or act that threatened or affected his interests. Such was his knowledge of affairs about him that the belief grew among the turbulent men that the admiral was a wizard. The most absurd stories that he was taking the entire squadron by diabolical contract direct to the dominions of Satan, became current morsels of gossip.

On October 8th and 9th, the mutinous portions of the crew became united and a plot was laid to force the commander into a quarrel. A riot was to ensue in which the admiral would as if by accident be thrown overboard. In this desperate situation, after all expedients had failed to satisfy the dangerous malcontents, from some unknown source came the compromising promise that if land were not discovered in three days, the expedition would be abandoned and all would turn about and set sail for Spain. Juan Marido was active in persuading his companions to be satisfied with this promise, and the proposed mutiny was thus averted.

Some claim that Perez Matheo, one of the pilots, told this story to Oviedo, the historian, who, not doubting that Columbus had been thus weak willed, made it a part of history, although no other writer of that time gave it the least credence or support. However, within the stipulated period land was reached and Columbus became one of the greatest heroes of all time.

With the triumphant return of the great navigator, and his magnificent reception in Spain, began the intrigue and persecution that finally resulted in sending Don Francisco de Bobadilla to be his judge and successor in Hispaniola. Armed with extraordinary powers, this representative of the king set sail with two caravels and arrived at San Domingo August 23, 1500. Columbus was then at Fort Conception, endeavouring to bring the lawless colonists and soldiers of Hispaniola to order. Bobadilla assumed control at once and made all the malcontents of the island his immediate counsellors and friends. The exaggerated testimony of every seditious and factious subject who could say anything evil of Columbus was taken with greedy unction, and the community became a cauldron of turmoil.

At the first morning mass after the arrival of Bobadilla, while the people were assembled about the church, Bobadilla ordered his royal patents to be read, showing his absolute authority, and he boasted that Columbus would not only be sent home in chains, but that neither he nor his lineage would ever govern there again.

In the midst of the excited throng a voice cried out: "Woe! woe! to the unjust judge!" Bobadilla was furious, but the bold accuser could not be found.

When Columbus arrived at the town of San Domingo, it was ordered that irons at once be placed upon him, and he was confined on a caravel in the bay. The charges which were drawn up against him were preposterous, even for that ignorant and bigoted age, but they were witnessed and signed by everyone who had been offended by his impartial discipline, or who hoped thereby to gain favour with Bobadilla. In the midst of this infamous court the clear cry again arose: "Woe! woe! to the unjust judge!" The indignant commander ordered diligent search to be made for the malefactor, but he could not be found.

With this overwhelming documentary evidence of oppression, sacrilege, fraud, incompetence, and treason to the king, Columbus and his two brothers, Diego and Bartholomew, were sent to Spain for trial.

Among the passengers on the returning vessels were several sailors who had been with the admiral on each of his three voyages, and they looked with horror on his treatment. One of them was Juan Marido, who prevailed upon the kindly disposed Villejo, in whose care the prisoners had been placed, to allow him to wait upon the afflicted discoverer. The drooping spirits of the great prisoner greatly revived by the inspiring attention of this common sailor, but he would not allow the sympathy of friends to remove from him any of the evidences of his sovereign's displeasure and ingratitude.

When they arrived at Cadiz and the facts became known, a great wave of indignation swept over Spain, and Juan Marido carried a long letter written by Columbus to Doña Juana de la Torre, who was the *aya* or governess of Prince Juan, and then the favourite of Queen Isabella. In this he explained the charges against him and described the treatment he had received.

Isabella was deeply pained at the injustice done the illustrious man. The two sovereigns wrote him an affectionate letter and ordered his immediate release. Eight thousand five hundred dollars were sent to him for his expenses, and he was invited to come at once to visit the royal court, then at Granada, where he was received with all his former distinction.

More than a year of weary waiting for the restoration of rights and privileges ensued, with nothing done but to recall Bobadilla and replace him by Nicholas de Ovando.

In the meantime, the peasants of Palos were surprised at the return of Merida, who had not been seen among them since she went ten years before to Santa Fe to set her mysterious visions before the queen. She was in frequent communication with Juan Perez and the physician Garcia Fernandez, the first friends and patrons of Columbus. They visited the Marchioness of Moya and held a conference with Isabella at Granada. The visions of Merida were against Columbus making another voyage. They showed nothing but suffering and peril. The admiral was past sixty-seven years of age, and his friends did not believe he could survive the hardships of another expedition. Every pressure was brought to bear to dissuade him from his purpose. The religious inspirations of Merida that had been so potent to help him to his first voyage were now as strongly used to turn him from the last. Nothing could avail against the courage and resolution of the old navigator. His friends sorrowfully saw him depart, as they believed, never to return.

On June 29th, Columbus arrived at the mouth of the river off San Domingo, Hispaniola. Pedro de Terreros, captain of one of the caravels, was sent to the new governor, Ovando, to ask permission to enter the harbour for shelter from an approaching storm. Ovando refused, and Columbus protected himself as much as he could by anchoring as securely as possible behind a promontory. Finding that Bobadilla and several others of his implacable enemies were about to set sail for Spain, he implored them not to leave the harbour until an approaching storm had passed; but, as they could see no signs of the predicted tempest, they scornfully rejected his warnings and sailed out into the open sea. Hardly had they left the bay, when a furious hurricane burst upon them. The two vessels containing the admiral's wretched foes went down with all their ill-gotten gain, and the others were so shattered as to be unseaworthy, excepting the one containing the confiscated property of Columbus, which pursued its way safely to Spain.

Denied entrance to ports over which his sovereigns had solemnly agreed to give him and his lineage forever the vice-regal control, Columbus steered westward, arriving at the mainland near Cape Honduras. Nothing but ill wind, misfortune and disaster ensued, until they reached the Gulf of Darien, when the disheartened crew with their battered ships turned back. Storms continued to beat upon the unseaworthy vessels; and, barely able to keep afloat, they put into Dry Harbor, Jamaica, on St. John's day, June 23rd. But, being unable to procure food, they sailed on eastward a few leagues exhausted and almost dying, to the next small bay, where the sinking vessels were run aground close together. They were lashed to one another, and an attempt was made to make of them a safe retreat from the savages that thronged the shore, as well as from the storms and pitiless sea. Here, broken by age, racked with pain, and confined to his rude bed in the half-sunken vessel that any hour might go to pieces or be destroyed by the untrustworthy savages, the intrepid admiral, his brother Bartholomew, and young son Fernando, fought their last battle with death in the New World.

The only hope lay in help from Ovando, who had refused him entrance to the harbour of San Domingo. But many miles of treacherous seas lay between him and the nearest civilized men, and the best means available for so perilous a voyage by a messenger, was the rude canoe of the natives. The task seemed impossible, but famine was imminent and any delay might mean the destruction of all. Some men with the required self-sacrifice and courage were found, and Columbus wrote his appeal for help. In a letter addressed to his sovereigns, he said: "Hitherto, I have wept for others; but now, have pity upon me, O Heaven, and weep for me, O earth! Weep for me whoever has charity, truth and justice!"

Days of weary waiting passed, and there was time enough for the messengers to have returned with help, but none came. In the common distress there were no spiritual advisers to infuse patience into the despondent men, or to hold them to obedience through religious fears, as the priests, who had started out with them, went ashore at San Domingo and had refused to proceed further. But there was a young man on board who had been with the stricken admiral on every voyage, and who had saved his life frequently through the most devoted and providential care. This young sailor, Juan Marido, passed among the discontented men like a soothing angel and quietly removed many of the irritations and rebellious ideas that fermented among the turbulent and feverish prisoners of the unwholesome wrecks. Every device was used to keep the riotous malcontents in order.

Their superstitious fears were for a long time influenced by marvellous visions that Juan Marido related to them with thrilling eloquence, and there were mysterious voices as they sat about the decks at night, warning them that disobedience to their commander meant destruction. Nevertheless, there came a time when the lawless could no longer be restrained. January 2, 1504, Francisco de Porras broke into the admiral's room, and, in a loud voice, accused him of keeping the crews there in order to see them perish. The mutineer declared that Columbus had no intention of ever returning to Spain. Reason and persuasion availed nothing, and with the cry, 'To Castile! to

Castile!" the two Porras brothers headed a mutiny of forty-eight of the strongest though most vicious men. Most of those who remained were helplessly sick, and the condition of the faithful ones seemed beyond hope.

But, however bad their situation, that of the deserters became worse. They rowed away in the canoes so laboriously secured by Columbus, and set out for Hispaniola. The boisterous sea buffeted them back, and they tried again, with such results that they concluded to abandon the attempt and to live by forage upon the natives. Like a pestilence they ranged through the island—destroying, robbing and slaying wherever they went—so that all supplies were cut off from the sick and despairing companions of the admiral. During this time Juan Marido was the only one who could go among the natives and secure the food that kept starvation away. His pious ministrations made them look upon him as a saint.

After eight months of indescribable anxiety for the fate of the courageous messengers to Hispaniola, a sail was seen late one evening coming into the harbour. The despairing sailors were transported with delight at the sudden hope of immediate delivery. The ship was from Ovando. It came alongside and hastily delivered a letter, a cask of wine, and a side of bacon. Then the commander, Diego de Escobar, who had been one of the most virulent enemies of Columbus, withdrew to a distance and expressed sorrow at the admiral's sore misfortunes. He offered to carry a letter to the Governor of Hispaniola, and Columbus hastened to write, imploring immediate help. Upon receiving the letter, Escobar at once hoisted sail and disappeared in the darkness of the same night. As distressing as this was to the miserable sufferers, it brought the confidence that their deplorable condition being known their speedy rescue must follow.

Juan Marido, in the kindness of his heart, obtained leave to go with a trusted companion to the lawless wretches who were still terrorizing the villages of the interior, in an attempt to restore them once more to order. A piece of the side of bacon was taken along as indisputable evidence that Escobar had visited the wrecks. Unconditional pardon was offered if the miscreants would at once return to obedience. Juan Marido and his companion had no difficulty in finding the marauders, but the overtures were scornfully rejected. Francisco de Porras assured the two peacemakers that his men were the lawful body and authority of the expedition, and that if any provisions had been sent in relief, his men must have them, either peaceably or by force of arms. The opinion, however, prevailed among the deserters, and was freely expressed, that if a relieving caravel had appeared, it was in truth only a phantom conjured up by the Italian wizard to deceive his confiding dupes, in whose suffering he was taking Satanic pleasure, and which he wished to heighten by false hope. The messengers sorrowfully returned and reported the new danger threatening them. In a few days their fears were verified by the report of a friendly Indian that the deserters were at the village Maima, near the harbour now known as Mammee Bay, about a mile away.

Juan Marido went again to persuade them to return to their allegiance and to abandon their unnatural menace to their more loyal brethren. Nothing would suffice. They were determined not only to possess themselves of all the stores of the loyal sailors, but to take the admiral captive and assume command. They at once marched forward in pursuance of their designs, and the sick commander sent his brother to meet them with all the force that could be mustered. It consisted of fifty pale and debilitated men. Six of the most muscular deserters agreed to make a combined onslaught upon Bartholomew Columbus. By his death they believed victory would be easy. One of them, known as Pedro Ledesma, had the voice and physical courage of a wild bull.

Just before the battle took place, he shook his lance at the peacemakers, who even at the last moment were trying to avert the fratricidal conflict, and boasted that six of those lances would be through the body of the Italian leader of fighting imbeciles in a very few minutes. Juan Marido divined the meaning of the boast and was able to get together half a dozen to assist and guard their leader. With loud shouts the deserters rushed upon the defenders, while the six *desperadoes*, led by Francisco de Porras and Pedro Ledesma, viciously attacked Bartholomew. The admiral's brother was a fighter and in his element. At the first shock four of the six confederates were killed, Porras was made a prisoner, and Ledesma was so nearly cut to pieces that he was left for dead in a ravine where he had fallen. In a sudden panic the cowardly remainder fled.

Although Ledesma had wounds enough to kill a dozen men, he recovered. On the next day the fugitive deserters surrendered themselves in the most abject submission. Four more months passed, and public indignation was so aroused in Hispaniola that Ovando, the governor, was compelled to fit out a ship for the relief of Columbus and his men.

Meanwhile, Diego Mendez, who had accomplished the seemingly hopeless task of crossing to Hispaniola as the messenger of Columbus, had exhausted all his resources to obtain help, and then set to work to collect rents from lands and property belonging to the admiral, in order to obtain the means of hiring a ship to go to the rescue. When he had succeeded and his boat was about to depart on the mission of long delayed mercy, Ovando hastily equipped a ship and put it under the command of Diego de Salcedo, who was the agent appointed to collect the rents belonging to Columbus in San Domingo.

Las Casas, the renowned priest, who was at San Domingo at that time, says that popular indignation arose to such a pitch that the conduct of the governor was denounced from the pulpits. The two ships arrived together, and the miserable crews were carried to San Domingo, where they landed on the third of August. The magnanimous admiral pardoned all the miserable miscreants who had caused him such distress during the long year of almost unparalleled suffering at Jamaica, excepting Francisco de Porras, whom he determined to take to Spain for trial. The two Porras brothers and Ledesma alone remained sullen and revengeful. Their chief hate was against the admiral, who, they claimed, had enticed them from Spain and plunged them into such dire misfortunes. Scarcely less was their hatred for Juan Marido, whose watchfulness had so often foiled them. That delicately featured youth, who seemed never to grow older, discovered the two irreconcilables in forbidden conference, and their enmity was greatly increased by the severer restrictions that were adopted toward them.

On September 12th, the sails that brought Columbus from his wrecks at Jamaica, were spread to carry him back to his ungrateful country. A tempestuous voyage ensued, and under cover of the storms Pedro Ledesma and Diego de Porras, the two sinister and revengeful characters on board, arranged a plan to slay the accuser of the seditious leader, who was left a prisoner at Hispaniola. However, the watchful eyes of Juan Marido seemed always to see any evil that was meditated against the great discoverer.

On the night of November 6th, as the shattered vessel lay off the harbour of San Lucar, between Palos and Cadiz, the watchman heard a cry and a struggle. Near the door of the commander's apartment, he found the admiral, who had been too weak to leave his bed during the voyage, bending over the unconscious body of Juan Marido. There had been a vicious blow on the head and a fatal stab near the heart. No assailant had been seen, and the mystery was deepened by

THE ADMIRAL, BENDING OVER THE UNCONSCIOUS BODY OF
JUAN MARIDO.

the unusual secrecy maintained over the stricken sailor. He was placed in the room occupied by the admiral's domestics, and his comrades were not allowed to see him. Several of these who had so long shared distress and misfortune with him, and believed in him as one inspired, were aroused to the greatest indignation at such an unnatural and cruel attack. Instinctively they saw signs of gilt in the sinister countenances of Pedro Ledesma and Diego de Porras, but this was forgotten in the joy that the end of their long suffering was at hand. The next day they went ashore to scatter over the country among their admiring and rejoicing friends.

Juan Marido was carried to the nearest convent and given over to the care of the nuns. Here there was continually some one of the sailors waiting about the gates, begging to know the fate of their beloved comrade.

In a few days the venerable Friar Juan Perez of La Rabida and the physician, Garcia Fernandez, came to the convent, bringing with them the aged mother of Merida. Two or three weeks passed, when one morning the sailor who had most persistently lingered about the convent, saw a procession issuing from the gates, bearing with the utmost tenderness and respect a covered litter, in which he believed lay the body, dead or alive (he could not learn which), of the friend who had so cheered and helped him through many months of despair and suffering. He followed them on to Seville and learned that his friend was dying, but could not die contented until the hands of the almost equally helpless Columbus had been laid in a parting blessing upon his head. A few days later the sailor saw his friend buried in the ground reserved for the nuns in the garden of the convent of the Sacred Heart. Then he learned that Juan Marido was Merida of Palos, whom he had known in their early childhood.

Las Casas, the venerable friend and historian of Columbus, says that Pedro Ledesma, the murderer of Merida, was some months later found dead in the streets of Seville with a dagger through his heart. Merida had left an avenger.

Ojeda

The Spaniards console themselves in their unfortunate experience with America that they have retired with honour and have taken with them the bones of the discoverer. However, with the rest of mankind there are grave historic doubts as to either of these claims being true. The tribulations, unrest and uncertainty connected with the removal of the illustrious dust of Columbus from place to place, serves to recall interest in the fate of the remarkable characters who thronged in his wake to the New World. In most of them the highest motive was that of the unrestricted passion for adventure and lawless conquest.

On the second voyage, Columbus had with him a man small of stature but sinewy as a leopard, whose extraordinary bravado and reckless daring exceeded them all. This man of romantic adventures was then only twenty-one years of age, and yet he had already made himself famous for his reckless exploits in the Moorish wars. He was a page in the service of the powerful Don Luis de Cerda, Duke of Medina Celi, when he made himself notorious as the dare-devil Alonzo de Ojeda.

Just before the fall of Malaga in 1487, during a desperate sally of Moorish cavalry, which surprised and put to rout his company while it was out on a gay parade, the youthful page Ojeda was made prisoner. He was taken into Malaga, stripped of his brilliant uniform, and given the inglorious task of attending to the stalls of the horses. Nothing, however, exasperated him so much as to see the horse that he had so patiently trained given over to a son of the captain, an unkempt imp of about his own age, with whom he had been compelled to exchange clothing. Luckily, he had a Moorish cast of features, and his despised clothing was ultimately much to his advantage.

A few days after his capture it happened that, while assisting to water some horses at a well just outside the city, the Moorish boy, clad in his soiled page's uniform and riding Ojeda's horse, came up to quench his thirst. Less than a mile away, Ojeda could see the white tents of the Castilian besiegers. A daring thought struck him, and with him to think was to act. With a running leap he sprang upon the back of his horse behind the Moorish boy, locked his arms around him, struck his heels into the animal's flanks, and called out to the horse the well-known words of command. Like an arrow the animal sped toward the distant tents. The howls of rage from the men who followed as swiftly as possible upon the remaining steeds, and the shrieks of the struggling Moorish lad, aroused all the horsemen on the plain, and, with the war cry of the prophet, they converged from every direction upon the flying animal and its writhing, twisting riders. Hearing the uproar, and supposing an assault of the enemy was about to take place, the Moorish cavalry in the city sprang to their horses, went with all speed to the plain, and formed in rank to resist a charge.

Such an array of horsemen led the Spaniards to conclude that the Moors were making a last mad dash for liberty. The call to arms resounded, and the eager Castilians were in a moment on their horses with poised lances, sweeping toward the enemy.

Supposing the oncoming Spaniards were the occasion of the alarm, the Moors stood their ground until driven back into the city by one of the most sanguinary conflicts of the siege. The best of the Moorish cavalry had fallen, and all hope of help from without being lost, the city at last surrendered.

The youthful Ojeda raced his obedient horse into the midst of the Spanish camp with his terrified prisoner, and a little later had the pleasure of riding at the head of the procession, resplendent in a new uniform, to witness the surrender of the city.

Five years later, a more romantic episode occurred to distinguish him at the siege of Granada. Through some means not now known, the Moors had made captive a Christian girl distantly related to Doña Beatriz, Marchioness of Moya, who then occupied a tent adjoining that of Queen Isabella. For a Christian girl to be taken by the Moors meant immediate slavery in one of the *harems*, a fate so abhorrent that it always called forth the most desperate expedients for rescue, and was the choice method of retaliation by the Moors upon the hated Castilians.

When Ojeda heard of the capture, his impetuous nature was at once aflame with the resolution to rescue her, although such a feat had been rarely accomplished.

LIKE AN ARROW THE ANIMAL SPED TOWARD THE DISTANT TENTS.

It is doubtful if the youthful daredevil ever laid any deliberate plans, but his first move in this case was to allow himself to be captured, presumably trusting to luck to keep his head on his shoulders and to find some way to escape captivity with the girl. At this time the Moors were too much occupied with the impending fall of the city to give the customary attention to prisoners. He was summarily manacled and cast like a piece of rubbish into one of the prisons adjoining the Alhambra. The city was full of distress, confusion, dissensions, and disorder. So much so that the score of Spanish prisoners with him were nearly starved to death from neglect. Having small hands and large wrists, he succeeded, as he expected, in removing the manacles, with but little difficulty.

Equipping himself in Moorish clothing, obtained from the prisoners, he waited until night, and, with a little assistance, performed the almost incredible feat of climbing like a cat up the corner of the stone prison. He removed a tile from the high roof, escaped to adjoining roofs, and then to the ground. His first care was to secure a rope, with which he returned to the roof of the prison, and, fastening it securely, let himself down among the astonished prisoners. One of them being of Moorish extraction, and having been brought up in Malaga, was particularly well fitted for the task in hand. Ojeda released him from his chains, and together they climbed the rope and escaped to the ground. The streets were crowded all night with distressed and anxious people, and the two escaped prisoners mingled freely with them.

The Spanish party that had been recently captured was so prominent that it was not long before a clew was obtained as to the place of their imprisonment. When morning came the two men found a lodging place and slept through the day. That night, strangely enough, they found that the girl and her mother were kept in a room adjoining, and communicating with the great mosque in the centre of the city. It was doubly difficult to communicate with them, since in the distressed state of the people, the mosque was crowded at all times with anxious worshipers. However, what Ojeda could not accomplish by some feat of strategy, he did by reckless boldness. Procuring some Moorish male clothing, he awaited an hour when there were fewest chances of anyone being in the room but the prisoners, and then braced himself against the door, exerting such strength that its lock was broken. If there were any observers, they were too much occupied with their own woes to give the incident any attention. He went at once into the room and reassured the cowering women by telling them that he meant to assist the young lady to escape and that her mother would doubtless soon be at liberty, as he was assured that the city could not withstand the siege but a few weeks longer. The girl hastily donned the clothing brought for her, and boldly walked out into the mosque and passed on into the street.

In order to throw pursuers off the track, he had instructed the mother to wait until she heard someone coming to the room, and then to cry out that her daughter had been taken from her by an unknown person. He expected by this means to be able to escape pursuit until the supreme effort to get out of the city had been made. It was about an hour before daylight when the two men and the disguised girl reached the city wall at an unfrequented place. They waited patiently until the sentinel came to relieve the man on the wall, when Ojeda sprang upon him so suddenly that there was no outcry, took the ladder he carried, and mounted the wall. With a stroke of the poniard the sentinel who was to be relieved was silenced as quickly as the other. Although it had been a dark night, which favoured them so far, light was now breaking, and the utmost expedition was necessary. The ladder was drawn up and placed on the outside, when watchful sentinels, with keen ears, detected the unusual sounds, and called out their signals.

Receiving no answer, they approached, just as the fugitives reached the ground. With loud cries, the sentinels called to the squad of horsemen that patrolled the outside, while the fleet-footed prisoners sped away toward the Spanish encampment. With answering cries the horsemen came on, the clatter of horses' feet being heard from all directions. Bidding the girl run on, the two men, armed with the lances taken from the dead sentinels, covered her flight. Objects were visible but a short distance in the dawning light, when the first horseman to see them dashed upon them. Ojeda caught the horse by the nostrils, and, with a powerful jerk, brought it to its knees. At the same moment the other man ran the horseman through with the lance and dragged him to the ground. The two men then mounted the animal and sped on ahead of their pursuers, to the girl, whom they snatched up behind them. A minute later they were safe among the astonished Spaniards.

Las Casas relates that he knew Ojeda when he was renowned as having been in more personal quarrels, fights and feuds than any other man without ever having been wounded or having lost a drop of blood. Ojeda attributed this immunity to a religious talisman which he always wore about his neck, consisting of a small Flemish painting given him by his patron, Fonesca, the Bishop of Badajoz, who was a bitter and relentless enemy of Columbus, and did that great man more injury than all other evil influences combined. Herrera says that in the most dangerous situations, Ojeda would fasten the image of his military patroness to some object, calmly address his devotions to it, and then proceed with the utmost impetuosity to overwhelm his enemies.

The writers of that time have many anecdotes of his daring escapades. Las Casas relates one that well illustrates his reckless character. Queen Isabella, while in Seville, one day entered the tower of the cathedral. While looking out over the city from one of the balconies, she became aware that some object above her was greatly exciting the people far below her. Looking up, she saw to her horror that a man more than a hundred feet above her was dancing upon the end of a beam that projected about twenty feet from the structure. After holding the people almost breathless for several minutes, he walked back, placed one foot against the tower, and threw an orange to the summit. This was Ojeda, who became one of the greatest of Spain's early discoverers, and who founded the first settlement on the continent at San Sebastian, Darien.

His first extended experience on the sea was with the second expedition of Columbus, in which his irrepressible activity found exercise in every available enterprise of danger or hazardous exploit. Notably among these may be mentioned his search through the Island of Guadaloupe for nine lost sailors, and his visit to the interior of Hayti, which he believed to be Japan.

The little town of Isabella, founded by Columbus in Hispaniola, was seriously menaced by a warlike Carib *cacique* of the interior, known as Caonabo. This chief was surrounded by a strong and unusually well disciplined army in the midst of almost inaccessible mountains, but Ojeda proposed to take ten picked men and bring him a captive to Columbus. This wild project was in keeping with his love of extravagant exploits. In any other man such a proposal would have seemed ridiculous, but Ojeda had performed many a madcap feat equally hazardous and doubtful. He led his ten hardy followers over nearly two hundred miles of wild and hostile territory, to a place now called Maguana, near San Juan, where he found Caonabo preparing to resist to the utmost the establishment of the Spaniards on the island. In several previous conflicts, Caonabo had learned to respect the prowess of Ojeda, and now when the *cacique* saw that doughty fighter approaching him with all the deference shown to a sovereign prince, he was greatly pleased. Ojeda claimed that he had come to solicit Caonabo's friendship and to enter into a treaty with him. In a few days Ojeda had so ingratiated himself into the good will of the *cacique* that the chieftain agreed to go to Isabella to negotiate the proposed treaty. As a sign of perpetual friendship, Caonabo was to carry back with him the chapel bell of Isabella, which was the wonder of all the islanders.

When they were ready to start, Ojeda was surprised to find that the wily *cacique* was to be accompanied by a picked force of several thousand warriors. Ojeda inquired why he was taking such an armed force on a visit that was purely of a friendly character. The chief replied that he wished to visit his friends the Spaniards as became a prince of his power visiting in state such noble foreigners.

It became evident that nothing but a daring stratagem would effect the capture of the wily chief. The army marched on to the Little Yagui River, a branch of the Neyba, and halted for a period of rest. Here Ojeda produced a set of steel manacles, burnished till they shone like silver. He convinced Caonabo by a plausible piece of fiction that these elaborate shackles were royal ornaments worn by the Spanish sovereigns on occasions of great state. In order to dazzle Columbus with an insignia of such distinction and authority, it was advisable for Caonabo to pass through the royal consecrating ceremonies and then to wear the kingly bracelets. Thinking that this would confer upon him a special influence and authority over Columbus, Caonabo passed through an elaborate series of religious ceremonies, during which the shining bracelets were placed upon his wrists, he was set in front of Ojeda astride the horse, and the other Spanish horsemen gathered around them.

At a word from Ojeda, they struck their heels into the flanks of their horses and dashed away with their amazed captive. They had yet more than one hundred and fifty miles of thickly settled Indian country to pass through, in which all the people were either subject to Caonabo or were his allies. Ojeda and his men shunned the most populous districts, swept in a compact body at the highest speed through the towns, with the *cacique* in the centre, bound tightly to his horse, and kept their way as much as possible through the most unfrequented forests. After much suffering from hunger, anxiety and fatigue, they reached Isabella in safety and delivered the dangerous chieftain to Columbus.

Las Casas says that the Carib chief never deviated from that haughty and savage defiance so characteristic of the Indians. He would not pay the slightest heed or respect to any but Ojeda. It was the custom for all to arise when Columbus entered the room, but Caonabo refused to take any notice of his presence. However, Ojeda never came near him without the chieftain arising and saluting him with the profoundest respect.

Several attempts were made by the subjects of Caonabo to rescue him, but in every instance, Ojeda with a handful of horsemen put them to flight. A last effort was made by a brother of Caonabo with seven thousand unusually well prepared men. The battle was conducted with considerable skill, but the steel-clad horsemen went through them with irresistible destruction, and the dismayed savages fled, abandoning all hope of ever successfully opposing the invaders of their island. In the sporadic insurrections that followed, Ojeda added trained bloodhounds to his cavalry, and that savage terror was afterward used all over Spanish America for the extermination of the natives.

When Columbus returned to Spain, Ojeda returned with him, but did not embark in the third voyage, which brought the admiral back in chains. He was ambitious to lead an expedition of his own. As he had a cousin of the same name who was one of the first inquisitors of Spain, and who stood in high favour with the Spanish sovereigns, he had good reason to expect a fulfilment of his desires. Another powerful friend was Don Juan Rodriguez Fonseca, who was an implacable enemy of Columbus, and who had charge of all the affairs regulating the government of the New World. It was he who had given the small Flemish painting of the Virgin to Ojeda, which excited in him such religious fervour and headlong courage.

During the excitement occasioned by the letters sent back by Columbus from the early part of his third voyage, Ojeda easily obtained the equipment and authority desired, and he set sail from the port of St. Mary, opposite Cadiz, May 20, 1499. With him were Juan de la Cosa, who, next to Columbus, may be regarded as the ablest mariner of that day, and Amerigo Vespucci, the ruined Florentine merchant, whose name was given to the New World.

In twenty-four days he reached the continent at the coast of Guiana, South America, about six hundred miles south of the lowest point reached by Columbus. He passed on northward, destroying, as a diversion, the war-like inhabitants of one of the Carribee islands in several sharply contested battles, in which he had one man killed and

AN INDIAN VILLAGE REMINDING HIM OF VENICE, HE NAMED LITTLE
VENICE OR VENEZUELA.

twenty-one wounded. A month later he entered a gulf in which he found built an Indian village reminding him so much of Venice that he named it Little Venice, or Venezuela. Here he met with a singular adventure. As soon as the natives saw the strange objects sailing into their bay, they fled to their lake-dwellings, drew in the bridges that connected them, and appeared to be in the greatest terror. While the Spaniards were gazing at the village a vast number of canoes filled with men entered the harbour. The Spaniards tried to hold communication with them, but the savages rowed to the shore and fled into the woods.

In an hour some canoes came to the ships with sixteen girls, who were distributed equally, four to each ship, apparently as a peace offering. The people then came swarming about the ships in great numbers. Suddenly loud shrieks were heard from a lot of old women standing in the doors of the houses. The young women sprang overboard into the sea and swam like fish toward the shore. Concealed weapons were brandished from all sides, and a shower of arrows was sent into the ships. The Spaniards turned their cannon upon the temerarious natives and put them to ignominious flight. Two of the girls were recaptured, but they escaped the same night.

It is worthy to note that at the next place where they landed they enjoyed the most extreme hospitality. This was at a point supposed to be near where Maracaibo now stands. The people, and especially the women, were distinguished for their remarkable physical symmetry. They entreated Ojeda to allow a company of Spaniards to be taken into the interior, where others of their tribes could behold the marvellous visitors. Twenty-seven men were accorded this extraordinary privilege, and the Indians prepared litters, on which the delighted Spaniards were carried with all the savage pomp of ancient kings. When the cavalcade of royal arch voluptuaries reappeared before their envious comrades, they were followed by many thousands of rejoicing natives, who made the forests ring with shouts and songs.

It was here that Ojeda was so taken with the superior intelligence and beauty of a daughter of one of the Indian *caciques*, or chieftains, that he took her away with him, which, according to the Indian customs, made her his wife. He named her Isabel, and she had no inconsiderable part in his subsequent career.

It was also at this place where Ojeda wrote his account to Spain of meeting with an English fleet, of which there is no account in English history. It greatly excited the Spanish Government, and vigorous measures were at once taken to prevent the English from ever gaining a foothold in the New World, which they claimed as exclusively their own.

Without finding any sources of the wealth he sought, he went to Hispaniola, where his commission forbade him to land, caused a great deal of unnecessary trouble to Columbus, who was then at San Domingo, trying to bring order into his rebellious colonies, sailed on to Porto Rico, and there loaded his ships with slaves, which he carried to Spain and sold.

Although there were only about twenty dollars to each sailor in the division of the profits, yet the fame of Ojeda as a daring navigator was such that he easily obtained a fleet of four vessels for another voyage. The two partners in this enterprise who furnished the money went with him. They attempted to found a colony in Venezuela, but the expedition experienced nothing but disaster. The two partners put Ojeda in chains and set their sails for Hispaniola.

It had been their intention to leave Isabel, the Indian princess, who believed herself to be the lawful wife of Ojeda, on the mainland at Bahia Honde, but owing to the friendship of the sailors for her, she was smuggled on board and went with him to Hispaniola. Ojeda planned to escape, and when the *caravels* anchored near the shore of Hispaniola, Isabel assisted him one night to get down over the side of the vessel with the intention of swimming ashore. She was able to free his hands from the manacles, but could not relieve him of the shackles on his feet. He was nearly half way to the shore when he gave out and was compelled to call for help. A boat was sent out to bring the crestfallen prisoner back to the ship, but they refused to take in the Princess Isabel, and she was compelled to swim to the inhospitable shore.

Toward the end of September, 1502, the prisoner was turned over to the Governor of San Domingo. The case was carried to Spain, and about all that is known of what followed is that he was so restored to favour in 1505 as to be given the command of another expedition to America. Three years later he was destitute in Hispaniola, and was nursed through a severe fever by the faithful Isabel, who had maintained herself during the previous six years among the natives about San Domingo, and had come to him as soon as she heard of his arrival.

Ferdinand of Spain at this time decided that he wanted to send colonists to the Isthmus of Darien. Only two trustworthy men were available. One of these was the penniless Ojeda, the other was the rich and influential Diego de Nicuesa. The veteran pilot, Juan de la Cosa, used all his influence for Ojeda, and the King decided to divide the territory between them. They were made joint governors of Jamaica, and given equal authority in their respective territories. The richly equipped fleet of six vessels commanded by Nicuesa, and the three scantily fitted *caravels* furnished by La Cosa, arrived at San Domingo about the same time, where Ojeda was anxiously awaiting them.

Not satisfied with his equipment, he succeeded in persuading a lawyer named Martin Fernandez de Enciso, who had saved about ten thousand dollars in the practice of his profession, to join him and invest his fortune in additional equipment. Meanwhile the rival governors had embroiled the whole community in a fierce quarrel over their conflicting claims. Diego Columbus, then Governor of Hispaniola, settled the quarrel over Jamaica by asserting his own rights over that island. He sent Juan de Esquibel with seventy men to take possession and to hold the island against all comers. Ojeda swore by the image of the Virgin he wore that he would have Esquibel's head whenever he had occasion to visit Jamaica, and Nicuesa—no less angered—put in command of his men the chief enemies of Columbus.

Ojeda was remarkable for the noted men he gathered around him. On this expedition he had with him several who became famous, among whom was Francisco Pizarro, afterward the renowned conqueror of Peru. Hernando Cortez (the subsequent conqueror of Mexico) had engaged a place in the expedition, but was prevented from going by an inflammation of the knee. Among the crew of the ship taken to Ojeda's colony by the lawyer Martin Fernandez, was Vasco Nunez de Balboa, who, in 1513, discovered the Pacific Ocean, and in the relief vessel of Valdivia was Hernando De Soto, discoverer of the Mississippi, in 1542.

On November 10, 1509, Ojeda left San Domingo, and, after a short and prosperous voyage, reached the mainland at Cartegena, The veteran pilot La Cosa had been here with Bastides eight years before, and he warned Ojeda not to run any risks with the natives, as they were dangerous warriors. All of La Cosa's hard-earned fortune was invested in this enterprise, and he begged Ojeda to go to a more hospitable shore, where the natives were less ferocious and did not use poisoned weapons. Nothing appealed to Ojeda's sense of pleasure so much as the prospect of a hotly contested fight, and his sense of courage could not brook the thought of changing plans because of fear for a lot of naked savages.

When the ships came to anchor the shore was at once thronged with a host of hostile natives. Ojeda at once landed most of his force and ordered his friars to proceed with their religious ceremonies, preparatory to the conversion or annihilation of the Indians. In reply the unteachable savages brandished their weapons, yelled their defiant war whoops, and sounded their martial conches. Ojeda addressed a short invocation to the image suspended about his neck, and ordered a furious charge. The Indians were routed and hotly pursued twelve miles into the forest, where they made a determined stand, but were again routed.

The aged La Cosa fought with equal valour by the side of the impetuous Ojeda, but constantly warned him of the imminent peril of such an extended pursuit. Regardless of these wise remonstrances, Ojeda continued the chase until late in the evening, when they arrived at the village Yurbaco. The place seemed deserted, and the Spaniards, supposing that the natives had fled in terror at their approach, scattered among the houses in search of booty. A moment later the surrounding forest echoed with the whoops of warriors who poured in upon the surprised and disorganized Spaniards a bewildering shower of poisoned arrows. Each straggling body of men was surrounded by overwhelming numbers of the savages. In vain the desperate fight for life was heroically waged.

For every Indian killed there seemed to be a score to take his place. Ojeda and several of his men succeeded in getting into an inclosure of palisades, which enabled them to maintain themselves longer than the others. La Cosa, with a larger body of men, had fought his way outside the principal ring of battle, but learning of the peril of Ojeda, turned back to his rescue and succeeded in reaching the palisade gate, where all but one fell under the unremitting hail of poisonous missiles. Just as La Cosa was struck down, Ojeda rushed with the ferocity of despair into the thick ranks of his enemy, and cut his way through their lines. La Cosa, though fatally wounded, succeeded in getting into a house with several others equally wounded, and there the little band of Spaniards defended themselves until they began to die in great agony from the poison.

"Sally forth," said La Cosa in the midst of his agonies to the one man yet remaining unwounded, "and if it should ever be thy fortune to see Alonzo de Ojeda, tell him of my fate!"

This man, like Ojeda, by the impetuosity of his single assault, cut his way through, before the savages could concentrate their forces

IT WAS OJEDA, WITH HIS BUCKLER OVER HIS SHOULDER AND HIS
SWORD IN HIS HAND.

upon him, and these two were the only survivors of the seventy men who had continued the pursuit of the savages into the forests.

As the days passed without tidings from the pursuers, those on the ships became greatly alarmed. Scouting parties were sent out in all directions, but large bands of Indians everywhere drove them back. All attempts to find the missing men were about to be given up, when a searching party, passing by a mangrove swamp near the sea, saw the body of a Spaniard lying upon a tangled mass of roots. It was Ojeda, with his buckler over his shoulder and his sword in his hand. He was so weak that he could not speak. His buckler bore the dents of more than three hundred arrows, and, as usual, he attributed his escape to the Virgin patroness whose image he wore about his neck.

A few days later, while he was seeking to recuperate on shore, the squadron of Nicuesa, his late enemy and bitter rival, came into view. Ojeda was now at his mercy, and he sent some friends to tell of the great misfortune that had befallen the expedition and to discover what Nicuesa would do.

"Seek your commander instantly," cried the chivalrous Nicuesa, "and bring him to me. Myself and my men are at his service until the death of the brave and noble La Cosa and his comrades are avenged!"

In a few days four hundred men set out for Yurbaco. A short way out from the shore some of the men came across an object that made Ojeda more furious for revenge than anything that had yet occurred.

When the suspense over the fate of Ojeda had become most intense, just before he was discovered helpless on the mangrove roots, the faithful Isabel determined to set out alone to see if she could learn anything of the fate of her lord, trusting to her kinship with the Indians. Ojeda was much disturbed when he learned of the dangerous but loving mission on which she had gone, but all hoped for her safe return. The object which the advanced scouts brought so tenderly back, was the body of Isabel. She had been bound to a tree and her body literally filled with poisoned arrows. Ojeda kissed his image of the Virgin, and, laying his hand on the head of the faithful woman, swore that never again would he stay his sword in mercy to an Indian, a vow which not many weeks later was singularly broken.

The Indian village that had been so disastrous to Ojeda was reached some time after nightfall. The force of men was equally divided, and just before midnight, they approached silently from two sides upon the slumbering people. The chattering parrots that filled the trees, often

53

made just as noisy by some prowling animal, drowned all the sounds made by the stealthy steps and cautiously whispered commands of the approaching men. Orders were given to permit no Indian to escape, and to take none alive. The savages were so completely surprised that they could make little defence. The slaughter was complete. Not a man, woman, or child was left alive.

While ranging the village for booty, they found the body of Juan la Cosa tied to a tree, and so hideous from wounds and the poison that the soldiers would not remain the rest of the night in the gruesome place. After securing about thirty-seven thousand dollars worth of gold ornaments, they destroyed every vestige of the village.

Nicuesa went back to his ships the sworn friend of Ojeda, who now took the advice of the lamented La Cosa and sailed on to the Gulf of Uraba. A fort was built, but the incessant hostility of Indians with poisoned arrows still surrounded them and harassed them at every step. Famine added to their horrors, and it seemed that they would be able to survive but a few days longer, when Bernardino de Talavera and his lawless band arrived with a well equipped Genoese ship, which he had seized from its owner and crew at Cape Tiburon, on the western end of Hispaniola. The relief did not last long, and they were again in the midst of famine, when Ojeda determined to return to Hispaniola in Talavera's stolen ship, it being the only seaworthy one in their possession, in order to obtain help, and to see why Martin Fernandez had not come on with the promised supplies. Relying on the great service they had been to the colony San Sebastian, and upon the influence of Ojeda, Talavera and his crew determined to go with the ship.

Once at sea, the utterly incompatible characters of Ojeda and Talavera asserted themselves, and a quarrel ensued, in which Ojeda was put into irons by the crew. While not far from the coast of Cuba a violent hurricane came upon them, and Ojeda was released to help pilot the ship. Not long after, it was driven, a helpless wreck, upon the coast. The miserable men, now willingly led by Ojeda, set out along the wild and swampy shore for the eastern end of the island, in the hope of finding some way to reach Hispaniola. Their sufferings from famine and hostile natives, many of whom had fled from the terrors of San Domingo, were such that when they came to a village where lived the Cacique Cueybas, they sank to the ground exhausted, completely at the mercy of the Indian chief. So far from taking the opportunity for revenge, the *cacique* tenderly cared for them as long as they chose to remain with him.

Their only hope now seemed to be in reaching Jamaica, where there was a settlement established by Juan de Esquibel, whose head Ojeda had sworn to take off on his first visit to that island. But conditions were altered now, and Pedro de Ordas was sent across in a canoe with some Indians to solicit help for the wretched Spaniards.

While starving and exhausted in the swamps, Ojeda had vowed to his Virgin patroness that if he were saved from the impending peril, he would erect a chapel in the first Indian village, and leave his beloved image there for the conversion of the heathen. This he did, and Las Casas says that on a visit there some years later he found the oratory kept in scrupulous order, and the image held in such reverence that the Cacique Cueybas ran away with it for fear the good bishop might steal it.

When Pedro de Ordas reached Jamaica, so far from holding enmity against Ojeda, Esquibel at once sent a *caravel* for the unfortunate men, and cared for Ojeda at his own house. Ojeda was soon enabled to go to San Domingo, where he found that Martin Fernandez had already departed for San Sebastian with a ship load of supplies.

On hearing that Talavera and his crew were at Jamaica, Diego Columbus, in accordance with his strict ideas of justice, sent some men with an order for their arrest, brought them to trial, and hanged them. The testimony of Ojeda at the trial of Talavera and his men was largely instrumental in their conviction, and some of their friends resolved to assassinate him. One night, as he was going to his lodgings, he was set upon by a band of ruffians. His sword was out in a moment, with all his old-time vigour. Although assailed on all sides, he laid about so effectively that the midnight enemies recoiled and then fled, pursued by the valiant but prematurely aged warrior. Not one of them escaped without a dangerous wound to nurse as a result of their lawless temerity. From this episode on, Ojeda is named no more in the Spanish records. This man of amazing feats and romantic exploits became a monk in the convent of San Francisco, according to Gomera, and Las Casas says that, when dying, he asked to be buried in the portal of the convent, so that all who entered might tread on his grave.

Nunez

The throng of adventurers infesting the New World four centuries ago contained none whose achievements were more deserving of honour, or whose fate was more deplorable, than those of the restless gentleman of fortune, Vasco Nunez de Balboa, discoverer of the Pacific Ocean. Like others of the impoverished nobility of Spain, he took the first opportunity to sail to the land of promise in the belief that he could find unlimited fortune on its golden shores. Failing to get the desired reward in his voyage along *terra firma* with La Cosa and Bastides, he tried farming in Hispaniola, but succeeded only in getting so deeply in debt that he could not escape from his creditors when he sought to try his fortune on other voyages. At last an opportunity came which he determined not to lose. The Bachelor Martin Fernandez de Enciso was about to sail to San Sebastian, Darien, with supplies for Ojeda.

Notwithstanding his creditors, he determined to go. Stratagem was necessary, but a gentleman of fortune is not usually wanting in resources. When the vessel of Fernandez was well out to sea, a cask which had come from the farm of Vasco Nunez, and supposed to be a contribution of provisions for the colony, suddenly burst open, and the urbane Nunez stood smiling before the astonished Fernandez. The Bachelor was furious at being thus imposed upon, and swore that he would set Nunez ashore on the first land they touched. However, the accomplished and polished Nunez soon proved himself to be such a valuable recruit, that the oath of Fernandez was never carried into execution. A more remarkable destiny was in store. At the harbour of Cartagena, while ashore repairing a boat, a *brigantine* came up, commanded by Francisco Pizarro, with about thirty men, all that remained of Ojeda's settlement, to which Fernandez was repairing with his supplies.

After considerable persuasion, Pizarro and his men agreed to return, and San Sebastian once more received its colonists, but they were again speedily reduced to starvation. Vasco Nunez suggested the happy expedient of possessing themselves of a prosperous Indian village which he had seen on the west side of the Gulf of Uraba when he was on the voyage with Bastides. As soon as possible San Sebastian was abandoned for the new land of promise. The village was found, the Indians were dispossessed, and the promised wealth of provisions and spoils was secured, amid great rejoicings at their good fortune. The unhappy natives fought hard, but could not withstand their steel-clad foes, and so the famous Spanish town of Darien came at once into existence. All the country round was plundered, and fifty-five thousand dollars worth of gold ornaments was soon in the coffers of the colony. As Spaniards in those days were never known to live at peace with themselves or others, it was not long before the colony was rent with hostile factions, prominent in which was the rising leader, Vasco Nunez de Balboa.

In the midst of this trouble the boom of cannon was heard across the bay, and a vessel, which proved to be one searching for the settlement of Nicuesa, came into view. As the source of their dissensions was in the fact that Darien had been discovered to be just inside the territory of Nicuesa, a happy solution appeared in the proposition to send an invitation with Colmenares, commander of the *brigantine*, to Nicuesa, offering to him the governorship of the colony. But the condition of Nicuesa and his men at Nombre de Dios was worse than that of the colonists at Darien. He had lost by starvation all but a handful of his men, and when he appeared on the *brigantine* with his woebegone followers, the faction under Nunez refused to allow them to land. The unhappy Nicuesa begged to be permitted to live among them, even as a prisoner in irons rather than to be compelled to return to Nombre de Dios. At this Nunez repented and championed his cause, but the rabble forced him to depart. He sailed away for Hispaniola, and neither Nicuesa, the rival of Ojeda, nor his crew, was ever heard of again.

As Nunez was the only one who had shown him any friendship, Nicuesa, just before his departure, presented him with a powerful bloodhound, named Leoncico, which in the many tragic scenes that followed, became almost as famous in Spanish annals as his master. He always received a soldier's share of the booty; and, in this way, earned for Nunez nearly five thousand dollars. Hardly had Nicuesa

BEHOLD MY DAUGHTER, TAKE HER FOR THY WIFE.

left the harbour, when the man who had so humbly sailed away from Hispaniola in a cask, on the ship which Fernandez commanded, was recognized as the chief man in the colony. Fernandez was tried for the unlawful usurpation of authority in a territory outside of his jurisdiction, his property was confiscated, and he was imprisoned, but a little later allowed to return to Spain.

A few unfortunates having been left by Nicuesa to hold Nombre de Dios, Nunez sent two *brigantines* to bring them to Darien. On the return voyage, two Spaniards, who had fled nearly two years before from some punishment of Nicuesa, and had taken refuge with Careta, the *cacique* of Coyba, were picked up. Their story of the riches of their late host was eagerly devoured, and a plan was laid to ravage the territory of the chief. One of them went on to Darien to act as guide for a party of invasion, and the other returned to the *cacique* to assist in his betrayal.

In a few days Nunez set out for Coyba with one hundred and thirty men. The Cacique Careta hospitably received the Spaniards and set a feast before them. Appearing to be satisfied, the Spaniards left their host with many expressions of good will, but that night returned, captured the village, and took everything of value that could be found.

"What have I done," Careta asked, when brought before Nunez, "that I and my people should be treated so cruelly? Have I not welcomed thee and thy people as my brothers? Set us free and we will remain thy friends. Dost thou doubt me? Then behold my daughter. I give her to thee as a pledge of friendship. Take her for thy wife and be assured of the lasting friendship of her family and her people."

Nunez recognized the fact that it would be of great native ally. He therefore accepted the offer of friendship, and the Indian princess, according to Indian usage, became the wife of the Spaniard. Her quick intelligence, courage, and faithfulness made her his companion in many perilous enterprises, and his loyalty to her had much to do with his lamentable fate.

According to the terms of this alliance, the enemies of Careta were speedily reduced, and the spoils received amply repaid the Spaniards. While on a friendly visit to Comagre, a neighbouring *cacique*, the eldest son of the chief presented the Spaniards with four thousand ounces of gold and sixty slaves. A quarrel began over the division of the gift and developed into a general fight. In great indignation and disgust, the Indian prince struck the pile of gold to the floor with his fist and exclaimed: "If this sordid metal is indeed so precious in your eyes that in the hope of finding it you abandon your homes, invade the distant lands of others, exposing yourselves to such suffering and peril, I will tell you of a land where you may gratify your utmost wishes. Look to those lofty mountains in the south. Their streams run down through sands of gold into a mighty sea. The kings who reign upon its borders eat from golden vessels and drink from golden bowls."

The vast prospect afforded by this information was such as to change the Castilian adventurer into a world benefactor, inspired with the loftiest ambitions. He realized that if he found an ocean beyond the continent, it would cause him to be ranked among the greatest discoverers of the earth.

From the best information he could gather, the power of the chiefs through whose territory he must pass, was such that it would require a picked force of not less than twelve hundred men. Full of the grand purpose before him, Nunez returned to Darien and dispatched Valdivia to Hispaniola with the royal fifth of about seventy-five thousand dollars in gold for the king, and a letter to Diego Columbus, asking him to use his influence with the king to secure the necessary twelve hundred soldiers with which to make his way to the western ocean and conquer the fabulously rich kingdoms. The frail *bark* of Valdivia was thrown by a storm among the rocks known as the Vipers, off the south coast of Jamaica, where it went to pieces. The crew of twenty men escaped in a boat, but the storm drove them upon the coast of Yucatan, in the cannibal province of Maya. The unfortunate survivors, excepting nine, were sacrificed to the idols and then devoured by the savages. Five men and two women died natural deaths, and two, a priest and a soldier, escaped, the priest being rescued eight years later by Cortez.

The interval during which Nunez was waiting for the return of Valdivia was occupied with several romantic expeditions for gold, varied by savage war- fare against the hostile natives. The watchfulness and devotion of the Indian princess several times saved both Nunez and the settlement from disastrous conspiracies made by the surrounding foes, and such was the deadly determination of the crafty Indians to kill Nunez, that of forty who had been sent to assist in cultivating his plantation, everyone had been sworn to take his life. But Leoncico, the bloodhound, more terrible in his peculiar discernment, devotion, and bloody prowess than any Spanish soldier, was always prowling near his master, and not one of the Indians sworn to kill him had dared to lift a hand against him. On one occasion, when the factions in the settlement became unusually turbulent, Nunez left, ostensibly on a hunting expedition, but in reality to let them have the experience of their own injudicious control. Before daybreak he left the scene of his riotous countrymen and set out for the home of the Cacique Careta, with the Indian girl behind him upon a horse, and the great bloodhound, in reality a species of mastiff, carefully reconnoitring, as was his custom, both sides of the way some distance ahead. The vigilance, intelligence and prowess of this animal was such that Nunez was relieved of all fear of ambush or attempts at assassination.

Arriving at a small village about ten miles from Darien, he stopped with the chief for rest and food. Although hospitably entertained, he had no reason for any considerable faith in the friendship of his host. While partaking of the food set before them in the Indian's hut, a furious commotion was heard, mingled with the savage snarls of Leoncico. Rushing outside, they found the animal standing over the prostrate body of an Indian, whose throat was torn in shreds, while a dozen others were crouching together against the wall of the house, with their spears presented in defence, each fearing to throw his weapon, lest he become the next object of the animal's fury. In a few minutes at least a hundred armed men gathered round, vociferously demanding the death of the dreaded dog.

An untouched piece of meat lay upon the ground, near which a javelin was sticking in the ground. One of the dog's ears was slit and bleeding, as if the spear had barely missed its mark. These things Nunez quickly discovered, and, knowing that the animal never made an attack without cause, he acted with his usual promptitude. Seizing his host by the throat, he threw him to the ground and ordered the intelligent dog not to allow him to arise. Knowing that the least movement meant death, the chief lay prostrate on the ground, a terrified prisoner, while Nunez scattered the awed braves with his sword. After due investigation, he became convinced that an attempt had been made to kill Leoncico, which was doubtless to be followed by an attack upon himself. The chief and his men so strenuously denied this that Nunez allowed them to believe his suspicions allayed. The body of the slain Indian was ordered to be removed, the chief liberated, and the interrupted meal was resumed as tranquilly as if nothing had occurred.

While he was leaving the village, his princess drew attention to the fact that not an Indian warrior was to be seen except those of the chief's household. However disquieting this fact, Nunez relied on the sagacity of Leoncico to warn him of any immediate danger.

THE CHIEF LAY PROSTRATE ON THE GROUND, A TERRIFIED PRISONER.

Two or three miles from the village the dog suddenly struck a trail quite a distance from the main road and followed it rapidly. He had been taught to track nothing but men, and his excitement indicated that enemies were near. In a few minutes his prolonged but snappy baying not far ahead indicated that he had come upon his game. The forest was not dense on this part of the coast, and they soon saw an Indian in the lower branches of a tree, directly in the path some distance ahead. The dog was twenty or thirty paces away from the Indian and was walking back and forth in an open space, as if defying an unseen foe. Nunez stopped when he had drawn near enough to study the actions of the dog, while the Indian girl sprang from the horse and ran to speak with the Indian in the tree.

When she was halfway to him she suddenly paused, turned about, and started to run. At this, a score or more natives came from their hiding places and began to menace the dog with their weapons, while one caught the girl and attempted to carry her away. She had been taught to use the Spanish ladies' stiletto, and, drawing one from her cloak, struck her captor down at a blow. Nearly a hundred men were now between her and Nunez, and she stood with uplifted weapon, uncertain what to do.

Nunez called the dog to him and quickly strapped a kind of armour upon him, which did not impede his movements, but effectually protected his body, neck and head from the arrows and crude javelins of the Indians. He likewise covered his horse with a harness of mail, always carried for such an emergency. Just as this was completed, a shower of arrows rattled against his buckler. He drew his sword, sprang into the saddle, and at the word of command both horse and dog sprang eagerly forward to their well-known duty.

It was a hundred men to one, but savages were, even in such numbers, no match for the man who had the aid of both steel and beasts. These men had seen the Spaniards fight, and dreaded the ferocity of the beasts that helped them, but they believed that with such numbers, protected by their native forests, they could rid their country of this chief of the foreigners, and destroy the famous animals that gave him his power.

At the first charge of the horse, they ran behind trees and rained their missiles upon the approaching foes. Not the slightest effect came of their efforts, and one after another they shrank from the mouth of the dog, only to fall upon the still more fatal sword. At a signal the frantic assailants rushed upon Nunez and tried to drag him from his

63

horse. The sword flashed back and forth like a weaver's shuttle, and blood sprang from the throats and breasts of falling men. But even the dying clung to the Spaniard's legs, and he seemed about to be drawn to the ground, when the savage mouthings of the dog in front, accompanied by the flash of the woman's stiletto upon naked backs, opened a way and the horse plunged forward out of the bloody mass. But it was only for the rider to return to the charge, and in a moment more the battle of the naked pygmies against the steel-clad giant ceased. They ran howling in every direction, as if they were flying in helpless terror from some implacable monster.

Nunez was contented to let them escape, the armour was taken from horse and dog, the girl resumed her place behind him on the horse, and they went on to their destination.

Within a fortnight a messenger arrived in haste from Darien, praying Nunez to return and suppress the anarchy that had reigned since his departure. This was done, and then the evil news came that the Bachelor Fernandez had obtained at the court of Spain a verdict for heavy damages against Nunez, and that an order had been procured commanding him to repair at once to Castile to answer for the death of Nicuesa. His exalted ambitions were about to be struck down, and his brilliant opportunities forever lost. But the royal order had not yet arrived, and his only hope lay in taking advantage of the delay. He hastily got together one hundred and ninety of the most hardy and courageous men, a number of friendly Indians, and a score of bloodhounds, over which Leoncico was solemnly appointed captain.

With this force he set out September 1, 1513, to accomplish what he believed would be a difficult task with a thousand well-equipped horsemen. He went by water to the home of the Cacique Careta, who gave him guides and additional men. Careta's daughter refused to be left behind, and insisted on sharing the perils of the expedition with the Spanish chief, whom she reverenced as her husband according to Indian law. Leoncico marched at her side, as if conscious that she was in his special charge. In the perils of the forest and during the battles with hostile natives, Leoncico valorously performed his share, but he never forgot or neglected his mistress.

Half of the force were left to guard the *brigantine* and *piraguas* in which they came to the province of Careta, and with the meagre remainder, Nunez penetrated to the foot of the mountain range, beyond which lay the great discovery which was the object of his high ambition. Only sixty-seven Spaniards were able to take up the march

THE SUBLIME PROSPECT OF THE GREAT SEA INSPIRED HIM WITH THE MOST EXALTED EMOTIONS.

to the summit. After a night's rest the little band set forth at daylight, September 26, 1513. At 10 o'clock they emerged from the forest upon the bare top near the summit. Here Nunez advanced alone to an eminence from which his Indian guides told him the ocean could be seen.

The sublime prospect of the great sea inspired him with the most exalted emotions. He fell upon his knees and gave grateful thanks for having been made the humble means of such a glorious discovery. His followers were then called to share with him the gorgeous spectacle of sparkling rivers and gleaming sea. They were thrown into religious transports at the splendour of the scene and the glory of the achievement. In prayers, songs, and shouts of praise, they embraced one another and swore to live and die the devoted followers of Vasco Nunez de Balboa.

The commander then called upon all to witness that in the name of the sovereigns of Castile, he took possession forever of that sea, with all the islands it contained and all the shores it touched. A week later he succeeded in passing down the long mountain slope through the territory of warlike Indians to the shore of the sea. Wading into the water with his drawn sword, he declared that the ocean and all that it contained or touched was annexed forever to Spain, with all the appertaining kingdoms or provinces by whatever right or title, ancient or modern, in times past, present or to come, so long as the world endured, and until the final day of judgment of all mankind. It is a matter of curious comment that the last shred of all such Spanish claims vanished in the last year of the Nineteenth Century.

Two chiefs on different occasions told Nunez of the rich countries toward the south, and had he lived he would doubtless have been the conqueror of Peru, instead of Pizarro, who listened to the stories and profited by the downfall of his leader.

After ravaging all the territory within their reach and undergoing the greatest hardships, the adventurous band of Spaniards, with a vast quantity of booty, reached Darien, January 19, 1514.

Meanwhile the king, greatly incensed against Nunez, appointed Don Pedrarias Davila Governor of Darien, and so great was the desire for adventure in the new country that Pedrarias soon had two thousand men and a fleet of fifteen ships. He was ordered to proceed at once to Darien, take hold of the affairs of the colony, and try Vasco Nunez for his alleged crimes. Accordingly he embarked for the New World only a few days before the tardy messengers of Nunez arrived, bringing news of the discoveries and achievements that should have made him, next to Columbus, the idol of the Spanish nation.

When Pedrarias arrived at Darien, Nunez welcomed him with the full measure of respect and obedience. Like most Spanish Governors, Pedrarias desired to be free of all rivals, and he took the most astute course to that end. Nunez was too popular and powerful to be proceeded with harshly or hurriedly, and Pedrarias played the part of intriguing politician, a hypocrisy unknown to Nunez. Under the pending investigation, he was kept at home while important enterprises and expeditions were given to favourites of the governor. Seeing that he was to be thus ruined and his discoveries turned to the profit and honour of others, he secretly sent Andres Garabito to Cuba for the purpose of securing an equipment for an expedition across the isthmus from Nombre de Dios to the shores of the Southern Ocean.

If his plans had not been constantly defeated through the enmity of Pedrarias, in this period he would have discovered and doubtless conquered Peru, making allies and friends of the natives instead of using such cruelty and slaughter as marked the course of Pizarro. Nunez was remarkable for the respect and friendliness he inspired among the Indians. It was not long after he obtained full control over Darien that a Spaniard could go unarmed within a day's journey without the slightest fear of harm, but soon after the rule of Pedrarias began, the wanton cruelty of his partisans was such that, according to Las Casas, the people were at all times harassed with the most distressing alarm. Every tree seemed to shelter a deadly arrow, darkness brought forth a thrust of the javelin from every isolated spot in the town, and dark spots on the plains or distant hillsides became hordes of revengeful savages about to overwhelm them.

Meantime, Andres Garabito returned from Cuba with a ship and seventy men, equipped for the southern expedition. He hovered off the coast and secretly sent word to Nunez, but the watchful Pedrarias heard of it and forbade him, under arrest, from leaving the town. Garabito was compelled to go on to Nombre de Dios alone and disband his expedition.

Pedrarias saw that the popular power was steadily slipping from his grasp into the hands of Nunez. The Franciscan friar, Juan de Quevedo, who had come over with Pedrarias as bishop of Darien, although his constant companion and adviser, had been at all times the friend of Nunez. In this deplorable condition of the colony, the good bishop devised a plan which he fondly hoped would secure better government and bring peace to the disorganized and suffering community.

"Why drive a man to be your deadliest enemy," said the diplomatic bishop to the envious and vindictive governor, "when there is a way to make him your most powerful friend? You have in Spain several daughters, one of whom you can make his wife. Thus you will have a son-in-law who will bring prosperity to your family and whose achievements will redound to the splendour of your administration."

The wily peacemaker then represented to Nunez that further antagonism between him and the governor meant the ruin of both and the destruction of the colony. Accordingly, articles of agreement were drawn up, specifying that the governor's daughter, then in Spain, should be sent for at once and married to Nunez on her arrival in Darien. Nunez, now relieved of all impediments, believed the time had come for the realization of his dreams for the exploration and conquest of the fabulously wealthy nations of the south. He began this enterprise with the prodigious feat of transporting across the Isthmus of Darien the material for the construction of the *brigantines* in which he was to sail on the ocean he had discovered. This Herculean task caused Herrera to exclaim: "Only Spaniards could have conceived or persisted in such an incredible undertaking, and no commander in the New World but Vasco Nunez could have conducted it to a successful issue."

While at the Isla Rica, news came that Pedrarias had been superseded in the governorship by Lope de Sosa. As this might materially affect his plans, he entrusted Andres Garabito, his former agent to Cuba, with the mission to find out if it were true. Unknown to Nunez, Garabito had become his vindictive enemy for having been rebuked severely in return for some derogatory remarks he had made against the character of the Indian princess, who had remained with her father, Careta, since the expedition of discovery to the ocean. Before leaving on this last expedition, Garabito had written to Pedrarias that Nunez was too much infatuated with the Indian girl ever to marry his daughter, and that the agreement had been entered into merely for the sake of gaining time in the scheme to overthrow the governor.

When Garabito reached Acla, near Darien, he found that the new governor had died as his ship entered the harbour, and Pedrarias was more strongly intrenched in power than ever. He caused himself to be arrested on suspicion, and in a confession accused Nunez of treasonable schemes against Pedrarias and the king. Burning with revengeful enmity, the governor sent a friendly message to Nunez to return to Acla for an important conference, and at the same time ordered Francisco Pizarro with a strong force to meet him and take him prisoner at any cost.

Unsuspicious of any danger, Nunez set out for Acla, and as he neared that place, met Pizarro, who made the required arrest.

"How is this, Francisco?" he exclaimed. "Is this your accustomed greeting?"

In the trial that followed it took little trouble on the part of Pedrarias to secure a verdict of death. The friends of the great discoverer appealed to the governor for mercy.

"No!" vindictively returned the implacable Pedrarias, "If he has merited the verdict of death, let him suffer the penalty."

Accordingly Vasco Nunez and several of his companions were publicly executed in the open square of Acla.

It is said that the Indian princess was kept in ignorance of what was transpiring until she got a hint that Nunez was at Acla, in trouble. Inspired with all the anxieties of her faithful love, she started at once to help him. On entering the town, she saw his head upon a high pole in the public square. Wild with horror, she attempted to take it down, when she was shot by a soldier and her body thrown to the dogs.

Marina

A singular circumstance is connected with the ownership of the Philippines which turns attention back to the romantic conquest of Mexico. Although the Philippines were discovered by Magellan, their occupation for more than three centuries was distinctly the result of Mexican enterprise, as was that of California. Yet when Mexico obtained its independence it took California without question and laid no claim to the Philippines. The title of the American possessions lay in the hands of the Spanish sovereigns, and were no part of the integral territory of Spain.

Mexico itself was discovered through the enterprise of Velasquez, Governor of Cuba, who secured the preliminary equipment for Cortes and gave him his commission. Cortes severed his relations with Velasquez, and on his own responsibility made New Spain a princely gift to Charles V. The royal fifth which the sovereigns received in their own right was a kind of rental tax in the farming-out process, which fastened such leeches and cormorants upon the Spanish colonies.

The New World attracted only such adventurers as had no hope for fortune or glory in the vast European dominions of the Spanish monarch. Cortes was one of the most desperate of these, and when he set sail for Yucatan, most of his equipment and authority consisted in what he had seized by sheer audacity.

When Cordova returned from an expedition to Yucatan a few months previous to the expedition of Cortes, he told a curious story of the word Castilian having been frequently repeated very distinctly to him by the natives, but he could not understand what they meant. It was finally decided that some castaway Spaniards might be among them, and Cortes was instructed to make a reasonable search. Inquiry among the Indians at the Island of Cozumel, near the coast of Yucatan, confirmed this belief so much that a letter was written and an Indian prevailed upon to carry it to the alleged white captives, telling them to appear at a certain point on the coast and they would be ransomed. The Indian messenger hid the letter in his hair and set forth upon his dubious errand. Through the imperfect medium of sign language and the little Spanish learned by a Yucatan Indian brought to Cuba by Grijalva, no intelligent communication could yet be established.

Neither messenger nor captive white men appeared, and the fleet left the island. Not far away one of the vessels sprung a leak, and the fleet was compelled to return to the island. As they were again about to set sail, a canoe was seen approaching from the mainland on the other side of the island. One of the ship's boats was ordered to intercept it, surprise the occupants, and capture them. At the first sight of the Spanish boat, the Indians sprang into the water with such precipitation that their canoe was overturned. All reached the shore and hid themselves in the underbrush, excepting one, who stood on the beach and boldly awaited the Spaniards.

They noticed wonderingly not only his absence of fear, but that he had a bit of a stocking tied about one leg. A still smaller piece of European cloth was tied about his waist. From his neck there hung the tattered remnant of a prayer book. When their boat touched the shore near him he fell upon his knees, spat upon the sand, and rubbed some of the moistened earth upon his forehead and over his heart. Then he arose and tried to speak, but they could not understand his strange words. At last they distinguished the word Castilian, and they realized that one of their captive countrymen stood before them. He called his Indian companions to him, and together they were taken before Cortes.

"Which is the Spaniard?" asked the commander, unable to distinguish between them. The captive kneeled at his feet, and Cortes threw his cloak over the naked shoulders. But it was a long time before he could endure the touch of clothing or the taste of the Spanish food, and several days elapsed before he had recovered his mother tongue enough to make his story intelligible. It was then learned that his name was Geronimo de Aguilar, and that he had been a priest with Valdivia. Nearly nine years before they had been wrecked upon the Viper rocks south of Jamaica, and the entire crew, escaping in their small boat, were driven upon the coast of Maya, in Yucatan. Valdivia and all the others but the priest, Aguilar and a sailor, Gonsalo Guerrero, were sacrificed to the idols and eaten by the priests and worshipers.

Another account, perhaps more reliable, says that seven of the men

HE STOOD ON THE BEACH AND BOLDLY AWAITED THE SPANIARDS.

and the two women died natural deaths. However, the most generally accepted historian of this episode says that the two who escaped the sacrifice hid behind the smoke of the altar; and, while the priests were searching for them, escaped into the woods. They continued their flight until they came into the territory of another *cacique*, before whom they were taken by some Indians, and who made them his slaves.

Aguilar kept his priestly vows, but the chief, in curiosity, caused him to be tempted beyond all the trials of St. Anthony. Guerrero married into the chief's household, and in time became so renowned for his prowess in war that he was raised next to the *cacique* in authority and wealth.

Aguilar received the letter of Cortes in due time to reach the appointed place, but he hastened to Guerrero, who lived some distance away, in order that he, too, could have the glorious opportunity to return to his countrymen. To the astonishment of the priest, his companion in captivity refused at once to go. Aguilar pleaded in vain.

"Brother Aguilar," said Guerrero, "I have united myself here to one of the women of this country, by whom I have three children; and I am, during war time, as good as *cacique* or chief. Return to our countrymen. Go! and may God be with you. As for myself, I could not again appear among them with comfort. My face is disfigured according to Indian custom. My ears are pierced and my lip turned down. What would my countrymen say to see me in this attire! I could not endure their mirth. Only look at my children. What lovely little creatures they are growing to be. How could I leave them! Pray give me for them some of the glass beads our countrymen sent you. I will say they are presents sent to my children from my brethren in my fatherland."

Aguilar could not prevail over Guerrero's resolution, and was compelled to bid him a sorrowful *adieu*.

De Solis, the Spanish historian, in speaking of the refusal of Guerrero, says:

Guerrero, having married a rich Indian, by whom he had three or four children, excused his stay by his love for them, pretending natural affection, as a reason why he should not abandon those deplorable conveniences, which with him weighed more than honour or religion. We do not find that any other Spaniard, in the whole course of these conquests, committed the like crime; nor was the name of this wretch worthy to be remembered in this history. But, being found in the writings of others, it could not be concealed. His example serves to show us the weakness of nature, and into what an abyss of misery a man may fall, when God has abandoned him.

A heavy ransom of hawk-bells and glass beads was paid for the priest and he was free, but the interpreter so essential to Cortes was not yet provided, as Aguilar could speak only the language used in the limited territory of Yucatan. However, this pressing need was soon supplied in a most unexpected and romantic manner.

Cortes left Cozumel, went around the coast of Yucatan and landed his men at the Grijalva River in New Spain. With about five hundred Spaniards, two hundred Cuban Indians, twelve horses and ten small brass cannon, he marched on into the interior. The inhabitants fled before him until he came to the province of Tabasco. There his first battle was fought with the natives, and he accomplished their complete subjection. Among the presents which they brought to their conqueror were twenty slave girls, whose work was to grind corn with a stone pestle and mortar, which they carried constantly with them as a badge of their servitude. One of them was of such commanding presence, intellectual countenance and truly royal beauty that she attracted at once the attention of Cortes.

While trying to communicate with her by signs, she spoke some words that caused Aguilar to interrupt the commander in great excitement. He understood her language. Communication was thus established with the natives, and her remarkable story was learned. As it afterward occurred, she became a New World Joseph to her guilty people.

She was the only child of the *cacique* of Painala, tributary to the Montezumas. When she was quite young her father died and her mother remarried. By inheritance she was the chief of the territory, but a son being born to her mother, its step-father wanted it to become the *cacique*. In order to bring this about, it was necessary to dispose of the princess, and she was secretly sold to some Indians going into Yucatan. It was given out that she was dead, and the guilty ones expected never to hear of her again. Some years later she was sold to the Tabascans, who gave her to Cortes. The Spaniards could talk to Aguilar, he could interpret it to the princess in the language of Yucatan, and she in turn made it known to the Tabascans and Mexicans.

Thus the Old World was put into communication with the New.

Cortes was a handsome man, of the most pleasing demeanour, and the Indian girl soon loved him with a fervour and fidelity which made her the constant companion of his most desperate sufferings and perilous campaigns. Historians agree that without her, Cortes would never have been the conqueror of the Montezumas.

She readily accepted Christianity and was baptized under the name Marina, being the first Christian convert on the continent of North America.

"Beautiful as a goddess!" exclaimed Camargo in his history of the conquest, and all who saw her were unstinted in their praise of her dignity, kindness and grace. She was always faithful to the Spaniards, regardless of the shameful betrayal which Cortes imposed upon her unenlightened spirit. She was of incalculable service to the conquerors. Several times by her keen watchfulness and intelligent understanding of the natives, she saved them from disaster and destruction. Many Indian ballads sing her virtues, and Melinche, as she was fondly known to the Aztecs, is the familiar spirit of Chepultepec. In a little time she learned Castilian, and became the indispensable interpreter and secretary of Cortes. He never appeared in public without her by his side, and the only name by which he was known over all New Spain was Molinche, which meant lord of Marina.

After defeating the Tabascans, Cortes plunged onward through the hosts of warriors that disputed his progress. With every victory he increased his strength by making friends and allies of the conquered nation. Montezuma, at the height of Aztec glory and power, watched the coming of the strangers with gloomy foreboding, yet hoping that on the way they would meet destruction.

At Cholula, aptly called the Rome of Anahuac, because of its being the centre of the Aztec religion, a conspiracy was formed which meant inevitable destruction to the invaders. This was the last city on the road to the great capital where lived the lord of all New Spain, in unapproachable dignity and splendour. Every instinct of religion, home and nation made it imperative that the unappeasable strangers should be allowed to come no nearer to the capital, and a crushing conspiracy for their destruction was completed.

Marina, always alert, keen and resourceful, became suspicious that treachery was meditated. A son of one of the principal chiefs became greatly enamoured of her, and so caused his mother to go to Marina and prevail on her to leave the Spaniards, as the gods had decreed their destruction. As if in great alarm, Marina went to her room and brought away her most prized treasures. Then the chief's wife, in greater confidence, told her that twenty thousand of the emperor's best troops were encamped near, ready to join the Cholulans in a sudden assault upon the handful of Spaniards, who were hopelessly cooped up in the narrow streets of the city.

Marina returned to get the rest of her personal effects, during which she managed to give Cortes the startling news. She then returned for the purpose of securing more information from the confiding Cholulan.

With his accustomed promptness, the commander seized three visiting chiefs and caused them to confess, amidst their protestations of innocence, that the Cholulans were planning the destruction of their guests. This discovery was all the more alarming as Cortes, believing in the friendship of the Cholulans, had allowed himself to be quartered at a great disadvantage, where his accustomed tactics could not be employed. This showed that the natives began to understand the invaders. The multitudes might no longer be appalled by the unknown thunder of artillery. Heretofore the hosts in the rear of the fighting men heard the terrifying roar and saw the black clouds of smoke arising, under which their men fell like grass before the hurricane. Suddenly monsters half animal and half man came tearing through the broken ranks of their warriors, and the panic of a dreadful fear seized them as they fled from before such all-devouring monsters.

European discipline had taken advantage of every weakness, and unresisted butchery ensued as long as the slaughtering arms could lift lance and sword, or while there was a flying or grovelling foe to be seen. Closer contact, however, had shown the Spaniards to be only ordinary men, using superior skill and better weapons. Awe was no longer an ally of the invaders, and the natives had resorted to stratagem. Cortes learned that the time set for the attack on him was to begin as he started to leave the city, and while his men were separated in the narrow streets. A force of about forty thousand men had been selected for this purpose, and they were at hand ready for the command.

As if falling more completely into the trap, Cortes called the chief priests, through whom most of the important business was transacted, and told them that, being about to leave, he wanted to meet the chiefs to bid them farewell, at the same time asking to be provided with an escort of two thousand men.

The great public court where the Spanish troops were quartered was surrounded partly by high buildings and the remainder by a wall, through which there were three wide gates. Early the following morning Cortes placed his cannon on the outside of the gates, so as to sweep the avenues leading to the court, and drew up his men in order at the advantageous points. Hardly was this done when the chiefs appeared with double the men required and entered the enclosure. Cortes came up quickly to the chiefs, with Marina by his side, and through her accused them of the treachery they were about to commit. They were struck with awe and terror at the power which the white chief had to read even their thoughts.

"I will now make such an example of your treachery," said Cortes, "that the report of it shall ring throughout the wide borders of Anahuac."

This was the signal for the firing of an arquebuse, and in an instant volley after volley of guns and crossbows poured into the mass of natives in the centre. They tried to escape through the gates, but impregnable rows of lances thrust them back. They tried to climb the walls, but their bodies were only so much better targets for the Spaniards. Others tried to hide under the bodies of the slain, but the ruthless swords soon found them out.

Hearing the firing of cannon, the Tlascalan allies, who had not been permitted by the Cholulans to enter the city, bound wreathes of sedge around their heads, so that they could be distinguished from the enemy by the Spaniards, and furiously fell upon the forces guarding the entrance to the city. The slaughter proceeded like a conflagration, excepting for a strong force under the priests, which took possession of the great pyramidal temple. This force could be reached only by the ascent of one hundred and twenty broad steps running around the four sides of the lofty pyramid.

In the face of stones, darts, and blazing arrows, the Spaniards scaled the steps of the vast edifice, and, with the burning arrows, set fire to the citadel containing the Cholulan warriors. Quarter was offered to them, but only one man accepted it, the others perished in the flames or threw themselves over the parapet and were dashed to pieces far below. Hardly a native warrior was left alive, and the city was given up to unrestricted pillage.

Cortes had at all times expressed to the Aztec ambassadors the profoundest respect for Montezuma, so that when the Spaniards were nearing his capital, he prepared to receive them in a splendour that rivalled the Orient in magnificent ceremony. Marina rode by the side of Cortes, and by her eloquence and address, completely won the susceptible heart of the Aztec king.

The Spaniards had a saying, "*He has not seen anything who has not seen Granada,*" and yet all agreed that the Aztec capital was more magnificent than Granada. In the centre of this city of half a million inhabitants, Cortes, with all his men and allies, was installed by the unbounded hospitality of Montezuma. A Spanish historian states that if a single horse had been known to them, even as a captive in one of the great museums of the capital, many Spanish armies would have perished before the city could have been taken.

When Cortes decided that the easiest way to make himself master of the city was to hold the life of Montezuma in his hand, he found that the Oriental seclusion of the emperor furnished a ready opportunity. Quietly, and in such numbers as not to arouse suspicion, picked men stationed themselves along the street to the palace. Numerous others wandered into the palace, as if they were merely gratifying their curiosity. Then Cortes, with Marina, and five of the men most noted in the annals of the conquest, sought an audience with the emperor. A complaint was made that two Spaniards in a distant part of the empire had been killed by the emperor's orders. Regardless of his protestations, he was told that he must become a hostage with the Spaniards until the matter was satisfactorily settled, or his life would be instantly taken. Montezuma listened in horrified amazement.

"When was it ever heard," he exclaimed, "that such a great prince as I left his palace to become the prisoner of a handful of strangers within his own gates?"

Two hours had passed in the strange controversy, and the impatient Velasquez de Leon cried out: "Waste no more words! Seize the barbarian, and if he resists, let us plunge our swords into his body!"

With a face white as death at the angry words of the soldier, the monarch turned and asked pitifully of Marina what it meant. She explained as gently as she could that he must go with the Spaniards, who promised to treat him as became a king. To deny this and incur their wrath, doubtless meant instant death. The fervent appeal of Marina changed the resolution of her emperor, and he bowed his will to the inexplicable boldness of the irresistible strangers.

Marina was constantly tender and solicitous for the comfort of her sovereign. He came to look upon her as a daughter, and to rely implicitly upon her counsel.

After Cortes had the city well in his own hands, and Montezuma, with his nobles and chiefs, had taken the oath of vassalage to the Spanish crown, Marina joyfully carried the word to her sovereign that he was now a free man and could return to his palace. He did not do so, for the reason, it is said, that Aguilar immediately informed him that the soldiers were bitterly opposed to it. They believed that the captivity of the king kept the populace in subjection, and Montezuma, so anxious not to have repeated in Mexico the horrors of such a massacre as had deluged with blood their holy city of Cholula, preferred to be a prisoner.

But the storm broke at last with a demoniacal fury almost unprecedented in the annals of history. Velasquez of Cuba, whom Cortes had deserted in assuming complete command in New Spain, sent Narvaez with two ships and orders to arrest and supersede Cortes in authority. While the undaunted conqueror was gone to the coast on the famous expedition which resulted in the capture of Narvaez and the absorption of his entire command, Alvarado, the future conqueror of Guatemala, and soldier of fortune with Pizarro in Peru, was left in command at the Aztec capital. At this time the chiefs and nobles of Mexico and its tributaries gathered at a great annual religious festival. The Spaniards, for some cause never satisfactorily explained, were ordered to attack them. A slaughter followed, more horrible in all its details than that of Cholula. After the first recoil of horror, the frenzied people turned upon the Spaniards like ravenous wolves. Supplies were cut off, and the audacious invaders were lost unless help came soon.

Through the influence of Marina, in whom Bernal Diaz, the most reliable historian of the expedition, says he never saw weakness or fear, Montezuma was induced to mount the battlements and persuade his people not to storm the fortress. In this they obeyed him, but it was the last respect they ever paid to him whom they had reverenced and feared next to their gods.

At this time Cortes, triumphant over the enemies of his own country, and with the additional forces acquired from his capture of Narvaez, entered the city. Soon after the drawbridges on the causeways, connecting the island on which the city was situated with the outer shore of the lake, were destroyed, and one of the most desperate and relentless conflicts ever waged was begun.

Slowly the infuriated hosts, regardless of the bloody havoc wrought against them by sword and cannon, pressed closer and closer upon the wretched garrison. At last came the pitiable end of Montezuma. He

MONTEZUMA FELL INTO THE ARMS OF HIS ATTENDANTS MORTALLY WOUNDED.

was persuaded to ascend the central turret of the palace and advise his people to permit the Spaniards unmolested to leave the city. As he appeared, the war cries ceased, and many fell prostrate as before the presence of a god. He spoke only a few words in favour of leniency to the Spaniard, when reverence vanished, and the people were electrified with scorn.

"Base Aztec!" they cried. "Woman! Coward! The white men have made you fit only to weave and spin!"

Then a hail of missiles fell about him, and he sank into the arms of his attendants, mortally wounded. While the natives were paralyzed with the revulsion of horror at having slain him whom they had so feared and venerated, Cortez, at the head of a little band, assaulted the pyramid temple, from whose broad platform at the top a band of Mexican nobles were enabled to throw into the Spanish quarters a constant hail of arrows and stones. Up the broad steps the heroic band went in the face of the arrows, stones and beams that rained down upon them, while the cavalry fought the enemy away from the base of the temple and kept the way open to the Spanish quarters.

Both armies watched with fearful interest the death struggle going on to its finish far over their heads. Once they saw two warriors seize Cortes and drag him to the edge of the great platform. There was a moment of fearful suspense, when one of the Aztecs was flung far over the edge, his body rebounding from steps and platforms to the earth far below, while the other assailant sank down almost severed in twain by the commander's sword. In half an hour every Mexican in the monster edifice was dead, and the Spaniards, in their religious fervour, rolled crashing over the sides of the towering pyramid all the hideous, blood-covered statues, idols, and sacrificial stones.

A lull in the sanguinary struggle followed, and Cortes believed the opportunity favourable to make terms with the maddened populace.

With Marina at his side he mounted to the turret in the palace from which Montezuma had so mournfully addressed his desperate people. The clear, musical voice of the far-famed Indian girl secured at once the most respectful attention. But the plea she was given to translate was only that of reproach upon the Aztecs as being the cause of such fearful bloodshed, with the command for immediate and unconditional surrender.

"If you do not," was the conclusion, "I will make your city a heap of blood and ashes, and leave not a soul alive to mourn over it."

Their reply was startling enough: "We are all content if for every thousand Mexicans who fall there has been shed the blood of one Spaniard. Our city is thronged with warriors as far as your eyes can reach, and you will soon be in our hands. The bridges are broken down and you cannot escape. We mourn that there will soon be too few of you to glut the vengeance of our gods."

A volley of arrows from the infuriated Aztecs ended the conference.

The dreadful truth was fast becoming clear to the mind of every soldier. The only chance for life lay in fighting their way over the broken causeways to the nearest shore, more than a mile away. The night this was attempted is known in Spanish annals as "The melancholy night." The score of slaughter was reversed, regardless of the most heroic valour. Secretly and silently the Spaniards and their allies moved out of their quarters and passed along the deserted streets toward the nearest causeway. Suddenly the shrill scream of a woman broke the stillness of the night, made inky dark by the drizzling rain. Instantly echoing cries resounded over the city, and the hosts of warriors poured in upon the fleeing Spaniards. The long, narrow causeway was at last gained, when the shrill war cries of myriad assailants on either side in canoes were heard coming nearer and nearer.

Then there was poured upon the long, narrow line of Spaniards and their allies a storm of missiles. In the midst of the bloody conflict of this midnight procession, Marina and the women, armed with shield and sword, fought for their lives as valiantly as did the men. One Marie de Estrada is especially noted for the daring deeds she performed. In that desperate retreat there were many feats of heroism that rivalled the valour of the *demi*-gods of the Grecians. Two-thirds of the Spaniards and more than three-fourths of the Indian allies who had entered the city were dead, and the remnant was but a disorganized mass when the shore was reached. Not a gun or cannon was saved, and yet the exhausted men fought their way onward through two hundred thousand warriors, gathered a few miles away at Otompan, and arrived safely among their friends at Tlascala.

In the course of a few months the indefatigable and indomitable Cortes secured such reinforcements from ships and men sent by Velasquez to help Narvaez that he turned once more toward the capital of the Aztecs. The story of how he fought his way back into the city through myriads of natives, who cared nothing for life as long as they could inflict a wound, and the horrible process of the remorseless conflict, which reduced the city, as Cortes had threatened, to a pile of blood and ashes, wherein a quarter of a million people perished, all reads more like a wild Oriental romance than the pitiable truth.

Not satisfied with the complete prostration of Mexico, which he asked Charles V to call New Spain of the Ocean Sea, Cortes set forth on an expedition of conquest to Honduras, taking with him the indispensable and equally tireless Marina.

A strange occurrence then took place in her history. At the place now called the Lake of Peten, Cortes summoned to meet him all the neighbouring *caciques*, chiefs and rulers. When they were assembled, Marina came forward to speak to them in the name of the great conqueror to whom they had come to pay their homage. All present noted a marvellous resemblance between Marina and one of the visitors, who was queen-mother of the powerful Maya tribe. The frightened woman saw that Marina was her daughter, whom she had sold into slavery, and she believed that she had been brought there to meet the just punish of death for her unnatural crime. But the gentle Marina ran to her with all a child's affection, loaded the unworthy parent with caresses, and covered her with the jewels she wore. Marina implored her mother not to grieve for the fault committed so long ago, since it had redounded so much to the glory of God and the Christian redemption of Mexico.

Bernal Diaz says that he heard her tell her people that if she had been born chieftainess of all the provinces of New Spain, the only pleasure that she could derive from it would be that she could give them all to Cortes.

It was on this expedition that Cortes gave her away in legal marriage to a Castilian knight named Jaramillo, who was afterward standard-bearer of the City of Mexico. From this time on the name of Marina and the Aztec title of Malinche, given to Cortes, disappears from the Spanish annals. But it is known that the Spanish Government, in consideration of her distinguished services, gave her estates and pleasure gardens, both in the country and City of Mexico. One of the most famous mountains in New Spain was named for her, and a bronze equestrian statue of her now stands in the city of Pueblo. As mention is made during her lifetime of her grandchildren, it is likely that she lived to a good old age, recognized by all as one of the greatest heroines of Indian America.

The Land of War

Patriotic heroism is esteemed by most nations as the highest virtue of the citizen. Next to this in universal commendation is that of religious heroism. As the Spaniard has always combined both of these in a high degree, his nation has from this point of view many heroes with the most daring exploits to their credit.

Singularly enough, every nation believes itself to be blessed with the greatest heroes and the most heroic achievements. From the pioneers at Jamestown and Plymouth Rock to the last fight at Manila, the citizens of the great American republic read rapturously of courageous deeds, and exalt their heroes. But as romance, all this makes poor reading by the side of the extraordinary exploits recorded in the annals of Spain. But there is an infinite difference in favour of American heroism, if it is judged by its ultimate value to civilization.

No one can read of the matchless daring displayed in the Spanish conquest of America without being impressed with the conviction that the conquerors considered the subjugation of the natives of but little more importance than the extermination of each other in the constant feuds of rivalry. So much was this true in Spanish South America that this territory was generally spoken of in Spain as "The Land of War."

If Pizarro had governed his conquests according to his experience with Vasco Nunez, discoverer of the Pacific Ocean, instead of after the manner of the vindictive Pedrarias Davilla, Governor of Golden Castile, there would probably have been no "land of war" to distract and exhaust the resources of Spain.

That all the soldiers were not as devoted to such enterprises as their indomitable leader, may be inferred from some singular incidents.

Francisco Pizarro, Diego de Almagro, and the licentiate Gaspar de Espinosa, who was represented in all the transactions by the priest

Fernando de Luque, completed their compact for the conquest of the territory south of Panama, and took oaths of eternal friendship over the holy sacrament. The expedition was fitted out with enthusiastic fortune-hunters, and the coast supposed to contain the fabulous riches of which they had heard, was safely reached. As on a previous voyage which Pizarro had made southward, only swamps, desolate wildernesses, and pauperized inhabitants were to be found, but the sufferings on shipboard or land were forgotten at every contact with the natives, from the assurances they gave that it was only a little farther on to the land of countless gold.

The Spaniards moved along the coast toward the golden paradise, and saw increasing evidences of a higher civilization, but such numbers of warriors thronged the shores that the handful of adventurers seemed ridiculously inadequate for any kind of campaign. At last it was decided that Almagro should return to Panama for reinforcements, while Pizarro remained with the soldiers at the Island of Gallo. There was almost a mutiny at the prospect of being kept at that desolate place so long, and many furious letters were written home to friends. Almagro seized all of these and informed the men that no such letters would be delivered. However, the wit of a crowd of desperate men is not so easily foiled. Presents showing the richness of the country and intended to impress the people and officials of Panama with the importance of the expedition, were taken back in abundance, and the soldiers succeeded in concealing in a ball of cotton, intended as a present especially pleasing to the governor's wife, a letter setting forth their grievances in full and signed by them all. It concluded with the *stanza*:

> Look out, Senor Governor,
> For the drover while he's near;
> Since he goes home to get the sheep
> For the butcher, who stays here.

The letter was uncovered at Panama, and it produced a great sensation. The *stanza* was chanted all over Spain. It had such an effect that the governor would not listen to the golden promises of Almagro, but at once sent two ships to bring away the Spaniards at Gallo, who had meanwhile suffered dreadfully from the inability to procure food and because of the continuous storms. The vessels sent to take them home were hailed with rapturous shouts of joy, and the conquest of Peru was being balanced across the finger of fate. Pizarro at once asserted that

HE DREW HIS SWORD AND STRUCK A LINE IN THE SAND.

decision of character which proves the great leader for great achievements.

He drew his sword and struck a line in the sand east and west. "Friends and comrades!" he exclaimed, turning toward the south and standing on the northern side. "On that side are toil, hunger, nakedness, the drenching storm, desertion and death; on this side ease and pleasure. There lies Peru with its riches; here, Panama and its poverty. Choose each man what best becomes a brave Castilian. For my part, I cross to the south."

Ruiz, the pilot, and Pedro de Candia, a native of Greece, unhesitatingly followed him, after which eleven others crossed the line. To remain alone on this desolate rock in the ocean, waiting for the doubtful reinforcements of Almagro, was heroism. Without it, Pizarro's name would have been unknown and South America would have had a different history.

After seven months the governor sent a relief vessel, with barely enough men to sail it. It found the fourteen men on the Island of Gallo as resolute as ever, and instead of returning in the vessel, Pizarro put his men aboard and steered for the Peruvian coast. In the Gulf of Timbuez, a populous city was seen, and, as the brigantine approached, upward of ten thousand armed warriors lined the shore. Assurances of friendship having been established, Pizarro decided to send Pedro de Candia, the Greek, ashore for information. Dressed from head to foot in dazzling armour, and with a drawn sword, the athletic Greek stepped ashore and marched straight forward into the town. The people fled before him, and thronged the housetops, as if they were being visited by a *demi*-god.

As he approached the entrance, a jaguar and a wolf from the pleasure garden of one of the nobles were turned loose upon him to test his supernatural qualities. The jaguar fled, but, according to the Spanish historians, the wolf lay down and suffered him to touch it with the cross, a proof of the miraculous efficacy of that instrument. Inside the town, in the midst of the wondering natives, he set up a board as a target and shivered it with a shot from his musket. The consternation and terror caused by this exhibition of power were very gratifying to the white man's sense of superiority, and Pedro de Candia felt a pride equal to the reverence and awe of the natives.

When he returned to Pizarro, he had a wonderful story of temples lined with precious metal and magnificent gardens of artificial flowers and fruits done in gold. For this exploit the Greek knight and cavalier was made, by the Spanish emperor, master of the artillery. In the deadly feud that followed a few years later between Almagro and Pizarro, in which Spaniards fought each other with more fury than they did the Incas, Candia was found on the side of Almagro, but with what willingness may be inferred from the fact that at the battle of Chupas, the Greek was struck down by the sword of Almagro's son for the alleged treason of firing his artillery over the heads of Pizarro's men.

Coasting southward until indisputable evidence of the rich Inca Empire had been obtained, the vessel returned to Panama, and Pizarro went to Spain, to obtain the royal commission and the means to pursue the conquest. Early in 1530 he returned to Panama, bringing with him four brothers, equally ambitious and courageous. Most of the offices and powers were vested in himself, and from this arose the disputes between Almagro and Pizarro which at last resulted in their mutual destruction. Meanwhile it is hardly too much to say that their exploits rivalled any adventures known to romance or history.

Almagro remained at Panama to procure and forward supplies, while Pizarro went on to Peru and set out on his search for the golden Inca. His entire force consisted only of one hundred and six infantry and sixty-two horsemen. With this insignificant force he crossed the Andes into the centre of the great Indian Empire, and came to the camp of the Inca, where he was spending the winter with an army estimated at a hundred thousand men. Here he decided to effect the capture of the Inca, a feat more daring and desperate by far than the peaceable seizure of Montezuma by Cortes. But there were audacity and courage enough in those two acts to place them among the chief wonders of history.

It was on Saturday, November 16, 1532, when the Spaniards reached the summit of extraordinary exploits in America. Without molestation they had gone on through the passes of the Andes and emerged upon the plains of Caxamalca. As the Spaniards marched into this typical Peruvian city of adobe buildings, not an inhabitant was to be seen, although the number of houses showed at least ten thousand population. About four miles away, beyond a swamp, across which ran a narrow causeway, could be seen the countless snow-white tents of the Inca's army. So far from any possibility of help, surrounded by mountains in whose passes a few Indians could prevent escape, in the presence of an innumerable host, which, without doubt, desired their destruction, every soldier lost hope. Francisco Pizarro alone remained confident. In the wide halls of the houses opening upon the public square, he placed his horsemen in two divisions, one under his brother Hernando, and the other under De Soto, who was ultimately to become more famed for his discovery of the Mississippi River. Pedro de Candia, the Greek, was stationed conveniently in the fortress with his artillery, consisting of two small falconets. The foot soldiers were concealed in the nearest houses, ready to rush forth at a signal.

In this manner, Pizarro prepared his men to receive a visit from the Inca, whose long train of attendants they had been watching as they marched in admirable military order over the causeway. It was nearly sunset when the stately array filed into the great square, the Peruvian emperor borne upon the shoulders of a score of men. He was arrayed in gorgeous livery, and sat upon a throne of solid gold. Six thousand warriors entered the square, and not a Spaniard was to be seen by the natives until Father Valverde, a Dominican friar, came forward to the king, with a Bible in one and a crucifix held aloft in the other. The interpreter was at hand, and the astonished Inca sat upon his golden throne, held aloft upon the shoulders of his attendants, and listened to a doctrinal sermon that covered all essential points of belief from the creation to the papal bull that gave Peru to the Spaniards. The priest then advised the king to turn at once to the Christian faith and submit to Pizarro, who was the authorized representative of the great Catholic monarch, Charles V.

Enraged at such demands from the handful of strangers, Atahuallpa flung away the Bible which had been pressed upon him, and the priest, shocked at such irreverence, ran back into the nearest house, crying, "I absolve you. Set on at once."

Pizarro waved a white scarf, a gun was fired from the fortress, and the cry, "Santiago and at them," rang from every side of the square as the Spaniards, horse and foot, rushed with gleaming swords upon the compact mass of bewildered Indians. The two falconets and the few muskets had a broad target, and the thunders of their reports, with the dense black smoke that rolled upward from them, made it appear to the natives as if heaven itself had joined in the slaughter. Not a Spaniard was wounded, and not a single stroke in defence was made by the terrified Peruvians. So great was the pressure of the mass against one of the great stone walls, covering the space between the houses, that it gave way for a hundred yards, and through this space multitudes were able to escape from the slaughter-pen into the open plain, where the horsemen cut them down as long as their arms had the strength to plunge their swords. It was long a bitter saying among the Peruvians that the great wall was less cruel on that day than the Spaniards.

The longest fight was around the Inca, about whom his followers gathered and interposed their naked bodies, until it was long after dark before the royal litter could be overturned and the king captured.

Without doubt four or five thousand Indians were slain, this massacre being one of the foulest blots in all the dark history of Spain.

Soon after Atahuallpa had agreed to ransom himself by fining his three prison-rooms full of gold and silver to the amount of sixteen or seventeen million dollars, Almagro, Pizarro's partner, arrived with a welcome reinforcement of one hundred and fifty men and fifty horsemen, who clamoured to be led on to Cuzco, where stood the golden temple of the sun. The Inca was becoming a burden, although he had proven himself to be one of the most congenial and companionable of men. He learned to play at dice, and not only paid his lost bets, but always refused to receive anything in payment of the lost bets of others. No one ever attended him or did him a favour without receiving some handsome reward.

Two circumstances now appeared to hasten the end of the unfortunate King. Felipillo, the Tambuez Indian whom Pizarro had secured on his first voyage and educated as his interpreter and secretary, fell in love with the Inca's favourite wife. Rumours began to come in through Felipillo of a powerful avenging army being raised at the instigation of Atahuallpa. De Soto was sent on an expedition of investigation, but before he returned such abundance of evidence was taken by the secretary from Peruvian nobles visiting the Inca, that it was decided to bring him at once to trial. It is said that Pizarro was not averse to such summary proceedings, from the fact that the Inca held him in great contempt. This contempt of Atahuallpa came about through a singular circumstance. One day he asked a soldier to write the name of the Christian God upon the royal thumb nail. This was done and the Inca exhibited it to numerous soldiers, all of whom, to his delight, pronounced the same word.

But when it was shown to Pizarro he was silent. Neither Pizarro nor Almagro could read or write, and the Inca could not esteem the leader who was less informed than the follower. The trial for treason was held, and the Peruvian emperor was condemned to be burned, but by acknowledging the Christian faith his sentence was commuted to that of being garrotted. On the same night of the sentence, two hours after sunset, in the flare of torch lights, the judgment was carried into execution. A few days later De Soto returned with the information that he could not discover the remotest indications of an uprising; on the contrary, the natives seemed to be leaderless and utterly dazed. Not long after, Felipillo went with Almagro on an expedition to Chili, when he was unceremoniously hanged for a meddlesome intrigue. In confessing his sins to the priest, he said that he had manufactured the testimony on which the Inca was condemned.

Most of the gold paid for the ransom of the Inca had come from Cuzco, where there was said to be many times as much still untouched, in the temple of the sun. Almagro's soldiers clamoured for an opportunity to share in those fabulous riches, and Pizarro accordingly set forth for the capital of the Incas. This city, with an estimated population of two hundred thousand inhabitants, was taken without resistance, and not less than sixteen million dollars in gold secured as spoils.

Spaniards were then, as now, such inveterate gamblers that few of the soldiers could keep their gold longer than it could be gambled away. Leguizano, a horseman, was given the image of the sun as his share. It was a huge gold plate, bearing in the centre a head, from which extended sun rays. The first night he gambled away this magnificent prize, the story of which became so famous in Spain as to pass into a proverb, "Play away the sun before sunrise."

Leguizano was so disgusted that he left the army at the first opportunity and never touched a card again. Not long after he married an Inca princess and passed the rest of his life in trying to repress the rapacity of the Spaniards. In 1589 he wrote a long letter to King Philip II, enumerating the griefs of the natives and the crimes of the Spaniards. When he died he wrote in his will:

I pray God that he will pardon my grievous sins against the helpless people of Peru. I am about to die, the last of all the discoverers and conquerors. It is notorious that there are none surviving excepting me alone in all this country or out of it, and I now do all that remains to me to relieve my conscience.

Each soldier received enough of the golden spoils to make him among the richest men in Spain, but every division of the princely treasures only increased his avarice and greed. Adventurous leaders with small bodies of troops ravaged the country in every direction. One party under Sebastian Benalcazar set out for Quito, where, as the Spaniards were told, lay the greatest treasures of all Peru. Ruminagui, one of the Inca's generals, was governor there. Hearing of the approach of the Spaniards, he gathered his troops together and met the enemy, in a desperate conflict, on the plains of Riobamba. He could not withstand the mailed horsemen, and, retreating into the city, he set it on fire.

Meanwhile, his son Catuna had been busy day and night, removing the golden hordes of the temples to a place of hiding, after which the slaves who had carried the gold were killed. In escaping from the city as the Spaniards were entering, Catuna was climbing over a burning wall, when it fell upon him, and he was not only crippled for life, but frightfully disfigured. Here he was found by Hernan Saurez, one of the Spanish captains, who took a great interest in the youthful chief and treated him with great kindness. In after years, Saurez met with misfortune and was thrown into prison for debt. Catuna visited him and asked him to promise that what he was about to say would always remain a secret, and that should any suspicion ever fall upon Catuna, the captain would be his protector against the avarice of the Spaniards.

The promise was given, and the next morning Catuna smuggled into the hands of the Spaniard a golden pineapple, which liquidated the debts and liberated him from prison. Saurez had been noted for his extraordinary kindness and charity to the natives, and it was mainly through this generosity that he had lost his fortune and become involved in debt. Catuna had been a slave in the household of Saurez, but he now became his master's constant companion. Catuna asked him to put a smelting furnace in his cellar and to protect it from all intrusion. This was done, and Catuna told his master to visit the place every morning. He did so, and never failed to find an ingot of pure gold. Every cent thus obtained was spent to alleviate the miseries of the natives. When Saurez died, beloved by the Indians over all Peru, it was generally believed among the Spaniards that Catuna, known as the Indian imp from his horrible disfigurement, had furnished his master with the gold through some dreadful practices of black magic.

A trial was called, and Catuna boldly admitted that he had sold his soul to the devil in exchange for the secret of how to make gold. The judges demanded proof, and Catuna named the necessary conditions. These were readily granted, and Catuna produced an ingot of pure gold. The judges put the precious metal to the test, and, finding it genuine, divided it between them. More proof was demanded, and so convincing was the golden argument that the judges pronounced him not guilty. He was tried before other judges, with the same effect, so that it was found that he could not be convicted by a single judge in all Peru. In consequence he became so feared that none dared to oppose him, and while he lived there was justice to the natives about Quito, as far as it could be obtained under Spanish law, or through the greed of the Spanish judges.

It seems that the secret treasures of Quito were also known to a servant of Catuna's father, who, because of his known faithfulness, had not been slain with the slaves. When Catuna died this servant told the secret to his daughter, so that it might not be lost. Not long after her father's death, she fell in love with a Spaniard, who would not marry her, because it would make him lose caste among his countrymen. To recompense him she offered to show him more gold than he could ever use if he would allow himself to be blindfolded in passing to and from the place of concealment. He gave his promise, and, at the trysting place in the neighbouring cliffs, she blindfolded him and led him a long distance through devious ways to a spot where she took the cloak from his head and bid him look. He was in a long, narrow cave, partially lighted from a rift in the rocks above.

To his astonished gaze there was revealed the lost treasures of Quito. There were planks of solid gold too heavy for him to lift, images of the sun broader than he could span with his arms, llamas in full life size, which with all his strength he could not move, and many hundred pounds of massive ornaments. He sat entranced on a great throne of gold that had been the royal chair of state for the Incas, until the Indian girl reminded him that they must go. Loading himself with the precious metal, he started to leave the cave unblindfolded. She appealed to him for the love of her and the sacredness of his promise not to betray her thus. He had nearly reached the entrance with her clinging frantically to him and pleading with him to be true to her and to his word.

With an oath he cast her aside and quickened his pace. But he had mistaken her devotion and courage. She sprang like a leopard before him with a dagger raised over his heart. He felt for his sword, but it was gone. Then he remembered that before entering the cave she had told him that it was sacrilegious for a soldier to enter armed into the holy place where they were going. In his eagerness to see gold, he had dropped his sword as she desired. He measured her lithe form in the dim light, saw the fierceness of her eyes, and knew that he dared not disobey.

"Drop the gold," she cried, and he slowly let it fall. "Tie this cloak tightly over your head and move as I direct or this knife will cleave

SHE BLINDFOLDED HIM AND LED HIM A LONG DISTANCE.

your heart."

He obeyed, and she directed him forward. After a long distance had been traversed, he no longer heard her steps or her voice. He asked if he could take the cloak from his head, but there was no reply. Fearing to remove it, he walked on until some laughing comrades came upon him and began to ply him unmercifully with jests. His grave face silenced them, and he walked on alone to the town. He determined to find the Indian girl, and to that end spent several months in search, using every means at his command. At last he got a clew and trailed her into a distant part of the mountains. She refused to recognize him, and would not listen to his pleadings or promises. Then he had her arrested on the charge of concealing royal treasure from the King of Spain. She was put to the torture, but did not say a word or utter a cry. The next morning the torture was to be renewed, but when the officers went for the victim, she was dead. A bit of glass and a bloody throat told the story.

The ease with which Cortes and Pizarro overran Mexico and Peru is no more astonishing than the desperate heroism with which the Indians fought after their awakening to the character of the Spaniards. There were many Bunker Hills and many a Thermopylae among them.

The American colonies were rejoicing in the first fruits of their independence when the last of the Incas fought the last battle for the preservation of his race. This was Tupac Amaru, a handsome and stately man, who passed through the length and breadth of the ancient empire, labouring with admirable eloquence and courage to alleviate the miseries and mitigate the wrongs of his countrymen. Not the slightest impression could he make upon the relentless masters, who exhausted the substance and lives of the people like vampires. He was a far-seeing man, and he satisfied his conscience by first using to the utmost all known means but that of force to save his race from judicial annihilation. He knew that the year 1780 was too late to achieve independence from his oppressors, but he believed himself able to secure by force what he could not get by reason.

With consummate skill he organized an army of six thousand courageous soldiers out of the dispirited and ragged natives. Half of them were armed with guns and the remainder with pikes and slings. Two hard fought battles, one of them continuing through three days, then took place, in which Tupac Amaru was victorious over nearly an equal number of well-equipped Spaniards, having a full equipment of cavalry and artillery. He then issued an address to the Spanish nation, offering complete submission if he could be assured of certain reforms that would give his people some measure of justice.

Antonio Areche, the *visitador* sent to quell the rebellion, replied that immediate and unconditional surrender was the only means whereby he could soften the torture which would be ultimately executed upon him and his followers. All available Spanish forces were rapidly concentrated, and a war of extermination followed. In a decisive battle the native army was almost destroyed, Tupac Amaru was captured, and the entire nation driven into the fastnesses of the mountains. The natives were hunted like wild beasts, but Spanish historians say that it cost the conquerors more than eighty thousand lives.

On May 15, 1781, the last of the Incas was led into the great square of Cuzco, and to him was read the sentence which is the most fiendish known in the annals of human history. It ordered that his wife and eldest son, with all his kinsmen, even to the remotest relationship, should be slowly tortured to death before his eyes. Even the smallest details of the diabolical cruelty were minutely specified. This Satanic orgy was to end, with the concentration of all the cruelties, in the torture of the Inca. His property and that of all his kinsmen was to be confiscated, their houses burned, and all documents, papers and books or records referring in any way to the Incas or their empire were to be destroyed, that all knowledge of them might be wiped from the earth. The customs and manners of the people were henceforth unlawful, and any one so offending the majesty of the law should be sent to the mines for life. The native language was forbidden, and it was unlawful for anyone to speak or write of the Incas or of the former history of the Peruvians.

Almost to the hour, one hundred and seventeen years before Spain was compelled to relinquish her last grasp on the western hemisphere, this hideous judgment was literally executed upon the pitiable remnant of the Peruvian people. But inaccessible portions of the Andes contained independent bands that continued the war of extermination until the Creoles became strong enough to drive Spain from South America.

In view of the heroism and horror of the Spanish conquest, it is interesting to note what became of the conquerors. All of them perished miserably. De Soto died of a fever in the swamps of the Mississippi River. Diego de Alverado was poisoned at his home in Spain. Hernando Pizarro lay in a Castilian prison twenty years for having caused

"WHAT HO!" HE CRIED, "YOU TRAITORS! HAVE YOU COME TO KILL ME
IN MY OWN HOUSE?"

the execution of Diego de Almagro, who had been the partner of the elder Pizarro in the conquest of Peru. Almagro's son, who took up his father's cause, was defeated, captured, and executed by Vaca de Castro, who had been sent from Spain to settle the quarrels of the conquerors. Pedro de Alvarado, who had also been with Cortes through Mexico, was killed by the fall of his horse. Gonzalo Pizarro, who made himself master of all Peru and who could have made himself king, as he was implored to do by Carbajal, temporized with Spain until he was captured and beheaded. Carbajal, who had been one of the bravest generals in Spain and one of the greatest monsters in America, was drawn to execution in a basket tied to the tail of a mule. Valverde, the priest who gave the signal for the massacre of the followers of Atahuallpa by Pizarro at Caxamalca, was killed by the Puna Indians. And so they all perished miserably.

But the most pitiable end of them all was that of the great conqueror, Francisco Pizarro. He had left the followers of his vanquished partner, Almagro, who were known as the men of Chili, to be reduced to the utmost straits of poverty. Although they were scattered over the country, they were united by the undying desire for vengeance against the men who had encompassed their overthrow. The bloody feuds that had made Peru and Chili known over the world as the land of war, still possessed them. At a time when Pizarro believed himself so secure in power that he could ignore the conspiracies of his enemies, nineteen men of Chili, sworn to secure the rights of Almagro's young son and restore their own fortunes, entered Pizarro's house about midday, with the unconcealed intention of taking his life. The old conqueror, not having time to buckle on his armour, bound a cloak around his arm and swung his sword with all the old-time vigour.

'What ho!" he cried, "you traitors! Have you come to kill me in my own house?"

Two of the conspirators fell under the blows of the sword, when the leader pushed one of his men upon the dangerous weapon, and, as it entered his body, the others sprang forward and brought the old man dying to the floor. "Jesu, have mercy!" he cried, making a cross on the floor with his bloody hand. As he stooped to kiss the sign, someone threw a heavy jar in his face, and thus died the conqueror of the Incas. So pitiable was his fate that, as Gomarra, the Spanish historian, says, 'There was none even to say, 'God forgive him.'"

Where the Spaniard Could Not Conquer—A Story of De Soto

A remarkable similarity is found in the wretched fate of the great Spanish discoverers and the fruits of the misrule that followed the Spanish conquerors. The tracks of the English, French and Spanish explorers crossed several times in the New World, and in every instance the experience of the Spaniards with the Indians was unique.

This was notably the case in the expedition that discovered the Mississippi River. The Spanish conquerors met a very different enemy in Florida than they had known in Mexico, Central or South America. Although the northern Indian was less advanced in the arts claimed by civilization, yet the broad territory known as Florida, became a continual burying ground for all who attempted to enrich themselves at the expense of the natives, distinguished as the North American Savages.

In 1521, eight years after Juan Ponce de Leon had discovered Florida, he returned to the coast on a conquering expedition with three vessels. At the first landing, all of his men were killed excepting seven, who, though so badly injured, succeeded in reaching Cuba, where all died of their wounds. Seven rich men of San Domingo, a year or two later, went to Florida for slaves. They succeeded in inducing large numbers of the natives to visit the ships, when the Spaniards weighed anchor and sailed away. Only one of the ships reached Hispaniola, and that without a single Indian, as all had either committed suicide or deliberately starved themselves to death.

In 1524, Vasquez Lucas de Aillon undertook the role of conqueror. He succeeded in getting back to San Domingo with about one-tenth of his men, most of them afterward dying of their wounds. Five years later Pamphile de Narbeaz entered Florida with three hundred men.

99

After hardships of the most incredible character, six survivors succeeded in reaching Mexico.

But the most notable of all for picturesque incident was the romantic expedition of Hernando de Soto in 1539. Not contented with the enormous fortune he had amassed in the conquest of Peru, he desired to become the Pizarro of North America. Emperor Charles V made De Soto Governor of Santiago, Cuba, and governor-general of the territory to be conquered. De Soto then fitted out the expedition at his own expense. He had married the daughter of Pedrarias Davilla, who had been betrothed to Vasco Nunez de Balboa, and she sailed with him to his new *marquisate*. De Soto's wife was thus the granddaughter of the Marchioness of Moya, who was so long the intimate friend and companion of Queen Isabella, and the unfailing friend of Columbus.

As they approached the harbour of Santiago, a typical incident occurred. A troop of horsemen came racing down to the shore, beckoning wildly and calling out "Starboard, starboard!" at the top of their voices. The ships turned as directed, and in a few minutes the horsemen began to beckon for them to turn in the opposite direction, calling out as wildly as before, "Larboard, larboard!" The ships turned just in time to escape being dashed to pieces upon the rocks. As it was, De Soto's vessel sustained severe damage, and the passengers were so alarmed that they escaped to the shore in their small boats. It was then learned that the Governor of Santiago, in great alarm, believing the approaching fleet to be French *corsairs*, had sent the horsemen to the shore to decoy them into a channel of sunken rocks. This fear of French *corsairs* had been occasioned by a combat, very singular according to modern ideas of naval warfare, which had taken place ten days before in the harbour in full view of all the people. No more striking contrast is possible in the history of sea fights than the ones that took place at Santiago de Cuba with the French in 1538 and with the Americans in 1898.

Diego Perez, of Seville, was the owner of a goodly ship, with which he trafficked among the islands. He had just entered the harbour of Santiago for the first time, when a French rover made his appearance through the narrow channel into the open bay. The Spanish historian of that time says that he knew little of Diego Perez, but his conduct showed him to be of a valorous and noble soul.

When the Spaniard recognized the presence of the Frenchman, he also recognized that under those circumstances it was his duty to fight.

A TROOP OF HORSEMEN CAME RACING DOWN TO THE SHORE.

Accordingly they came together and fought until nightfall. When they could no longer see to strike at each other, they agreed that no gentleman would fight with cannon, as there was neither courage nor honour in the use of such a weapon. Then they sent their compliments to each other with their most distinguished consideration, and made bountiful presents of fruits, wines and other delicacies. They agreed to fight only in the daytime, as became men of honour. Nevertheless, they kept sentinels posted to prevent any stratagem. At daybreak the fight was renewed and continued until each was exhausted with hunger. After refreshing themselves and complimenting each other on the valour of their men, they fought again until night. Then they visited each other, with many presents and with remedies for the wounded.

Great crowds of frightened people sat on the shore and watched the progress of the battle, nearly every one having all the money he possessed wagered on the result. During the second night of the conflict, Perez wrote a letter to the people of Santiago, reminding them that he was fighting their battle. If he won, he would have the Frenchman's ship, which would be reward enough for his labour, but if he failed the Frenchman would have his ship and there would be no return for his loss, which was already considerable. He told them that it was worth a great deal to have the sea purged of such a formidable *corsair*, whom he was now trying to sink for their especial accommodation. Under such conditions he deemed it only fair that in case he lost his ship they should render to him or his heirs its value. In that case he was ready to triumph or die. But the people ridiculed his request, saying that as he had to fight or die anyway, they could not see why they should be called upon to insure him against losses that would be due to his own weakness or cowardice.

Regardless of this ingratitude, Perez resolved to obey the dictates of honour and conquer or die, that his nobleness of soul might not be called into question. But the Frenchman, seeing that he could not leave the harbour with honour, resolved also to conquer or die. Thus they fought several days, enemies as long as they could see to fight, and convivial friends at night. At last Perez noted that his enemy seemed to be weakening, and he challenged him, according to the rules of war, to begin the battle on the next day and to continue it until one of them should be overcome. The Frenchman agreed, as if delighted with the prospect of a speedy victory, and after an evening spent in great hilarity with the Spaniard, he departed to his ship, agreeing that one or the other should not live to see the coming night.

When morning came the Frenchman was nowhere to be seen. The bay was sounded to see if he had sunk, but as no trace of the vessel could be found, it was conjectured that he might have sailed away in the night to secure help from companions that were probably not far distant.

When the fleet of De Soto appeared, the people were sure that it was a French fleet come to sack the town, because the Frenchman had declared, when he heard that the ungrateful inhabitants would not agree to recompense Perez, that if he survived he would bring a fleet and destroy the town composed of such ungrateful wretches. The horsemen hurried to the shore as if to welcome their friends, thus hoping to lure the Frenchmen to their destruction upon the hidden rocks. Happily, they discovered in time that it was their new governor.

So rejoiced were the people that, according to the historian, there was nothing in the town for a long time but sports, balls, feasts, and masquerades. In the meantime the natives, seeing so many Spanish soldiers coming into their unhappy country and realizing that nothing but the crudest slavery was before them, began to commit suicide in appalling numbers. The historian says that in one village fifty-six families made away with themselves in one week.

At the end of May, 1539, De Soto landed in Tampa Bay with two hundred and fifty horses and an army of a thousand of the gayest and most buoyant Spanish cavaliers that ever entered the Indies. About six miles inland they came to the capital of the Indian chief Harriga. The historian says that he had a bitter hatred against the Spaniards because he had been deprived of his nose and ears by Ponce de Leon, who had also given the chief's mother to the dogs. Harriga sent the women and children to places of safety, and assembled his warriors for a desperate resistance to the invaders.

After several severe skirmishes, the Spanish cavalry saw a small body of Indians advancing boldly toward them, with no appearance of hostility. Nevertheless, the horsemen charged furiously upon them, and all fled but one, who stood in the path with folded arms. The nearest horsemen were about to strike him down with their swords, when he threw up his hands and cried: "Brethren, I am a Christian. Slay me not, nor these good friends, to whom I owe my life."

The astonished cavalrymen lowered their swords and reined in their horses. The friendly Indians were recalled, all were taken up behind the cavalrymen, and brought into camp. There a curious story was told.

Ten years before, one of the ships that had been left behind by Narvaez, while searching along the coast for him, saw some Indians on the shore waving a letter. However, the crew were so afraid of the natives that they would not approach the shore until hostages were sent to the ship. Four Indians then came aboard and four Spaniards were sent ashore. No sooner were the Spaniards in the hands of the savages than the Indian hostages sprang overboard and swam ashore. Then the four Spaniards on shore were taken before the chief who had suffered so grievously at the hands of Ponce de Leon. The ship, in great alarm, sailed away, as it then contained hardly enough sailors to manage the vessel.

All the tribe assembled to take part in the torture of the captives, and the four men were brought forth to run the gauntlet of clubs and stones. One was only a boy, scarcely eighteen years of age. When he was led into the ring, the wife and daughters of the chief begged for his life. They pointed out that he could only have been a child when the chief suffered his unprovoked injuries. In answer Harriga pointed to his disfigured face and to the charnel house that contained the bones of his mother.

Here and there the Spaniards ran in the wide circle of howling savages, trying in vain to escape the deadly missiles. Presently Juan Ortis, the boy who had so engaged the interest of the chief's family, fell, seriously wounded. Then the eldest daughter of the chief begged her father to give the young man to her as her slave. At last, when the people were considerably appeased by the amusement they had enjoyed in torturing the others to death, Harriga consented, and Juan Ortis was led away by the girl. But his troubles had only begun. Whenever there was any special gathering of the chief's friends, he entertained them with a special spectacle of tortures for the youth, until he would have killed himself except for the kindness and encouragement of the Indian maiden. At last she secured for him the post of guardian over the charnel house, where the dead were deposited.

This onerous duty carried with it the injunction that if any of the bodies were disturbed by beast or man he should be burnt to death. One night he heard an animal at the body of a child that had been brought the previous day. He ran to the spot, but the body was gone. Realizing that a horrible death was certain to follow as a punishment for this neglect, he ran frantically into the woods, praying to his patron saint not to abandon him in this misfortune. Presently he heard a sound similar to that of a dog crunching a bone. Stealing forward in the shadows, he saw a gaunt timber wolf in a moonlit place, feeding upon the body. With a prayer to the Virgin, he launched his javelin, and then fell upon his face and prayed till morning. There he was discovered by the parents of the child, who had come to pay to its body the last rites. A few steps away they found the dead child, and by it the wolf transfixed with the spear. The whole village praised his courage, and petitioned Harriga to mitigate his severity with the Spaniard. But the chief declared that the white man was a constant reminder of the injuries he had received at the hands of his cruel nation, and that at the next festival the hated slave should be tortured to death.

Juan Ortis, now seeing nothing before him but a horrible death, decided to kill himself. As he was meditating one night in deep despair over the desperate fate that had overtaken him, and was thinking mournfully of the terrible contrast between his present condition and the hopes he had when he sailed away from his people in Spain, he heard a light step behind him among the dead in the gruesome charnel house. The moon had just risen, and the shadows were so deep that he did not recognize the chief's daughter until she was at his side.

"Listen to me," she said, softly, "and have the courage to do as I say. Tomorrow night at this hour a man will tap three times on the rear wall. Follow him at a distance without a word, until you come to a bridge twelve miles away, and you will be safe." She further explained that the guide would then give him a talisman, which he should carry to Mucoso, a neighbouring chieftain, who loved her, but who was an enemy of her father. The guide would show him the path which led to the capital of Mucoso, about twelve miles further on. As soon as he saw Mucoso he must give that chieftain the talisman and implore his protection from Harriga. No more could she do; for the rest he must trust to himself and his God.

Ortis was so overcome at her kindness that he fell upon the ground and kissed her feet. At this demonstration of gratitude, she left him, saying, "Do as I bid you, and travel only at night."

Ortis feverishly awaited the hour that promised him escape. At the appointed time the signal knocks were heard, and he followed the guide, gliding northward silently through the forest till they came to the boundary bridge. Here the talisman, which was to insure the favour of Mucoso, was given him, and the way he was to follow pointed out.

The following day he remained hidden, and the next morning he approached near the village of Mucoso. A crowd of Indians saw him and were about to kill him, when he showed them his talisman and called for their chief. He was then brought before Mucoso, who heard his story and received the gift. The chief was so pleased with the confidence of the princess who had sent the white slave to him, that he took Ortis into his own household and treated him as a brother.

Harriga was furious at thus losing an opportunity to revenge himself for his injuries. He demanded the return of the white slave, but, regardless of many injuries inflicted in consequence upon his people by the angry Harriga, Mucoso never betrayed his trust. Hearing that a number of his countrymen had landed on the near coast, he set out at once to seek them.

It was several days before Ortis could make himself understood in Spanish, as his ten years of captivity had almost deprived him of the use of his mother tongue. De Soto was greatly pleased, as it insured him an interpreter and a faithful adviser concerning the customs and habits of the Indians. Having gone naked so many years, it took a month of painful usage before he could endure to wear the suit of black velvet given him by De Soto.

The story of the wanderings of the explorers from the time they left Tampa Bay until the miserable remnant of less than one third arrived in Mexico, is interesting chiefly to the historical student, excepting for a few typical incidents and remarkable adventures. The man who had been so conspicuous with Pizarro in the conquest of Peru, found that his experience and fortune were unavailing against the unexpected courage, power, and patriotism of the unconquerable North Americans. The rich and enlightened natives of Mexico and Peru, however great their numbers or however bold their stand, became panic-stricken at the first sound of guns and the charge of the cavalry, but the North Americans stood their ground and launched arrows that pierced bucklers and mail with the power of bullets. Frequently they fought until the last man had been cut down by the sword, a weapon against which they had no defence. The Spaniards could never have overcome them nor governed them. It took a hardier and more judicial race to dispossess the North Americans of their homes and lands.

From the time the Spaniards landed at Tampa until they left the mouth of the Mississippi, in their frail boats, they were incessantly harassed by the furious and implacable natives. The Spanish historians relate with amazement many instances of unaccountable defiance and courage.

In one instance, while in Alabama, some advanced cavalry came upon a half dozen Indian hunters. Although these natives had never before seen white men or horses, they drew a line across the path and made sign to inform the intruders that if they dared to cross the line they were dead men. Astounded at such remarkable audacity, they dashed across the line and put the barbarians to the sword, but not until half of the men were seriously wounded and two of them dead. One Spaniard was pinned to his frantic animal with an arrow which passed through his thigh, pierced the saddle, and entered six inches into the side of the horse. Two of the horses had been killed with arrows driven entirely through their bodies.

After the battle with the Tula Indians, four of the foot-soldiers and two horsemen came upon an Indian hiding in a clump of bushes. The horsemen immediately rushed upon him with their swords. The savage did not await their attack, but sprang at them with an axe which he had captured in the late battle. His first stroke broke the descending, sword, crashed through the buckler, and almost severed the horseman's arm. Whirling about, he sunk the axe into the shoulder of the other horse with such force that the animal fell, throwing his rider forward, stunned, upon the ground. One of the foot-soldiers aimed a blow at the savage, but the axe met the descending sword and crushed the buckler against the man's shoulder so heavily that he was knocked breathless to the ground. The next nearest soldier was an expert swordsman, and as the Indian turned upon him the Spaniard delivered a blow with his sword which severed the red man's right arm, and the axe fell to the ground. The Indian then leaped upon his foe, trying to grasp the Spaniard's throat with his left hand, but the swordsman skilfully interposed his shield and nearly severed the body of his naked enemy with a downward blow of his keen-edged weapon.

The examples of individual heroism which the Spaniards so frequently met were, as they found to their sorrow, common to entire tribes, so that the wonder is that any of De Soto's men ever lived to tell the story. In the province of Vitachuco, ruled over by three brothers, the Spaniards met the most determined and systematic resistance. Vitachuco, the eldest brother, governed half the province. The younger brother warned Vitachuco that the Spaniards were the children of heaven, and therefore invincible. The elder brother replied that men who carried off women, plundered property, and lived upon the labour of others were traitors, robbers and murderers, who were more

THEY CAME UPON AN INDIAN HIDING IN A CLUMP OF BUSHES.

likely children of the devil. He reminded his brothers that having made themselves slaves of the invaders, he did not expect anything else of them than that they would praise their masters. He also admonished his brothers that men of merit and valour did not leave their own country to become brigands in other lands, make slaves of free-born men, and incur the undying hatred of those who were as brave and honourable as themselves.

The two brothers yielded, however, to the blandishments of the Spaniards, and Vitachuco found it necessary, in order to prepare a plan to overwhelm the invaders, that he should appear to do likewise. He sumptuously entertained the army in his capital four days, in the meantime assembling secretly ten thousand of his subjects, who hid their weapons in the neighbouring forest and entered the town bearing wood and provisions under the pretext of serving the Spaniards. With great skill he planned to invite De Soto and his men to witness a review of his subjects on an adjoining plain, at which the commander was to be seized upon a given signal, and the Indians were to draw their concealed weapons from their cloaks and annihilate the invaders. Doubtless the plan would have succeeded if it had not been necessary for Vitachuco to take into his confidence two or three of the interpreters who, in the hope of greater reward from the Spaniards, revealed the plot to Juan Ortis. He at once told De Soto and a plan was made to give the savages a lasting lesson.

Twelve Spaniards placed themselves in such a position that at a sign from De Soto they could seize the chief. The cavalry followed near and the infantry, in full readiness, marched on either side. Ten thousand Indians, apparently unarmed, were drawn up for the proposed review, in the form of a crescent upon the plain. The infantry and cavalry came rapidly into position for a charge before the Indians could realize the intention. Suddenly a musket was fired and before the Indians could draw their bows the cavalry was upon them with murderous sword-thrusts which found ready mark in the unprotected bodies. The infantry charged with a volley from their muskets and then rushed into a hand-to-hand conflict with their swords.

Vitachuco, though taken in complete surprise, fought like a snared tiger, killing two men before he could be bound. His followers fought not less furiously, but their bows were of little service in such a close conflict with the Spaniards' weapons. No valour could withstand so unequal a struggle and they fled before their relentless pursuers. Nine hundred of them, cut off from escape, threw themselves into a little lake nearby to avoid the deadly blows of the swords. The Spaniards, returning from the slaughter of flying Indians, surrounded the little lake and kept the swimmers out in deep water by shooting those who came near the shore. This continued from ten o'clock in the morning, but the desperate swimmers were not idle. Garcilasso, the historian of the expedition, says that three or four would swim abreast and another elevating himself upon their backs would send an arrow with such unerring aim and force that a soldier was almost invariably wounded or killed.

At night huge bonfires were built around the water and it was closely infested with watchmen, who shot all who attempted to escape. It was a perilous task, since numbers of the Indians swam near the shore in the shadows and then dived to the water's edge, when they would leap out, strike down the nearest man with their bows as clubs, and then endeavour to escape in the darkness of the woods. Few succeeded, however, as the bloodhounds usually brought down those the Spaniards failed to kill. When morning came such promises were made to the exhausted survivors that about two hundred surrendered. The others continued in the water until they had been swimming more than twenty-four hours, when all came ashore but seven young chiefs who could not be persuaded to surrender. At last, when it was seen that they were about to drown from exhaustion, twelve strong swimmers went in and brought them out unconscious, dragging them by the hair of the head. It was found that they were young chiefs, none of whom were over eighteen years of age.

Every Spaniard now had a slave and it was believed that the hostile tribe was so nearly destroyed that it would be the part of wisdom to offer Vitachuco his freedom on condition that he make peace with his captors. But the savage defied them, saying that he preferred death to their friendship. Nevertheless he was treated as a distinguished captive, and four of his domestics were detailed to wait upon him. Resolved not to live in captivity or slavery to the white men, he secretly sent word to all the captives that at a certain time while eating at the table with De Soto he would attempt to kill him, and that all who preferred death to slavery should, when his voice was heard, follow his example and attempt to kill their masters.

This time there was none to betray him. Seven days after his capture, as the chief and De Soto had just finished their morning meal, the Indian arose and bent his body backward, stretched out his arms and clenched his fists, beat his chest with such blows that the sounds could be heard half across the camp, uttered a bellow like a wild bull, and then leaped suddenly upon De Soto, bearing him instantly to the floor. The officers present sprang to the assistance of their commander, and sheathed a dozen swords in the back of the chief, but before this could be done De Soto had been struck so fiercely with the bare fists of the Indian that he was unconscious for half an hour. Blood flowed from his mouth, nose and ears, several teeth were broken, and it was twenty days before he could take the bandages from his face.

At the sound of the chief's voice, every slave without exception sprang upon his master. As few of them had any better weapon than their bare hands only four white men were killed, but all were sorely wounded before they could draw their swords and kill their assailants. In half an hour nearly a thousand Indian captives perished thus rather than to serve their captors.

After De Soto's death and his burial in the Mississippi, not far below Memphis, the survivors determined to make their way to Mexico. During a winter's work enough boats were constructed to hold them all and they embarked down the river which De Soto had named the Chucagua.

Scarcely had they set sail when the natives, who had never ceased to harass them while on land, now appeared, following them in boats as large and well manned as their own. The enemy's fleet continued to augment until there were more than a thousand boats. Although the Indians ventured no pitched battles, yet they made the night hideous with their songs and shouts, while the day never ended without the death of one or more Spaniards by the deadly arrows that almost constantly fell upon them. All the way down the long course of the lower Mississippi this dreadful pursuit continued until the Gulf was reached. Then with songs of joy and shouts of triumph for having driven away the pale-faced invaders, the pursuers turned back to their homes several hundred miles away, and the remnants of a proud Castilian army of invasion and conquest followed the shore for many weary weeks until they reached the settlements in Mexico—a pitiable crowd of spiritless beggars.

Adventures in Search of El Dorado

The sensation produced during the present generation by the discoveries of gold has caused vast numbers of fortune hunters to carry civilization to distant portions of the earth, which it would have taken ages to have peopled otherwise. These gold seekers came from among busy and prosperous communities. With such a condition in mind, it is easier to form a correct idea of the eagerness with which a nation of needy idlers just released from the excitements of war, would rush to the New World, which afforded unlimited opportunity for romantic adventures, and where incomparable riches were to be obtained in a day by the capture of temples, towns, Montezumas, and Incas.

Within fifty years from the first voyage of Columbus, Spain had overrun the whole of the Western Hemisphere south of the latitude of Northern Texas. The age of Argonauts, Phoenicians, and Hercules had suddenly returned to the Spanish nation. The most fabulous stories were readily believed, for fabulous things had actually been accomplished. Those whose imaginations were especially susceptible to the romantic, found a wide and fertile field in adventurous searches for the amazons and El Dorado. Both were largely mythical, but the belief in them was universal through two centuries, and they led to adventures unparalleled by such as Don Quixote or the heroes of the Grecian epics.

The currently accepted story was that a younger brother of Atabalipa had fled across the Andes, after the destruction of the Incas, with incalculable treasures, and founded a great empire. This emperor was variously known as the Great Paytiti, the Great Moxo, the Great Enim, and the Great Paru.

Pedro Ortez of Lima was lost on one of the expeditions into the mountains to the east of Cuzco and after a year reappeared with the sensational story that he had been captured and taken to Manoa, the capital city of the golden emperor. During the latter part of the journey he had been kept blindfolded, and after his escape he had wandered about lost in the forests so long that he had no idea how to return. The only relic he had been able to retain was a map of the city.

The wonderful capital was situated on three hills, one of which was of gold, another of silver, and the other of salt. The emperor's palace was supported by columns of porphyry and alabaster, and the galleries were of ebony and cedar. His throne was of ivory and the steps to it were of gold. Every detail was carefully marked out on a piece of white cloth by Ortez. He led an expedition in search of the city, but was unable to find it.

The historian Martin del Barco found a chief who had been on a friendly visit to Manoa, but would not betray its location. From this chief, Barco learned that the palace of the golden chieftain was made of marble. Its temple contained two towers twenty-five feet high, holding between them at the top a great silver moon. At the base were two monster silver lions secured by heavy gold chains. The immense gates of the palace were made of copper. In the temple was a sun of gold covering the entire eastern end. Here were kept in sacred seclusion the hundred virgins of the sun who, each morning at sunrise, anointed the emperor with a fragrant gum of great price and blew gold dust on him through reeds until he was thoroughly gilded from head to foot. This was all removed in his bath after he had partaken of his breakfast. From this custom he received the name of El Hombre Dorado, meaning the gilded man.

In 1595, Sir Walter Raleigh wrote a book entitled *The Great and Golden City of Manoa, which the Spaniards call El Dorado.* This he afterward extended by a history of the Lake of Parima.

Nothing was listened to in Europe or America with such avidity as stories of El Dorado. Southey in his history of Brazil makes the statement that the Spanish expeditions in search of El Dorado cost Spain more treasure than was ever received from all her American possessions. Among the most noted of these elaborate expeditions was one led by Balalcazar from Quito, another by Federmann from Venezuela, and another by Quesada along the way of the Rio Madalena. Orellana, whose name was for a long time given to the Amazon River, was one of the most persistent hunters for El Dorado, but like the searches of Diego Ordace, Berreo, and Martynes, a life was spent with no worthy results.

Curiously enough, the first extensive attempt to find El Dorado was set on foot by some rich merchants of Augsburg, Germany. Ambrosio de Alfinger, of Ulm in Suabia, was German agent at the Spanish capital for the Welser family and mercantile company. He secured a lease of Venezuela, then comprising the greater part of Northern South America. Within a year after the marvellous ransom in 1533, of Atahuallpa, Inca of Peru, the exploits of Cortes and Pizarro had penetrated, in the most brilliant and romantic colours, even to the lowest peasantry of the Old World, and Europe was wild with the gold fever. In the centre of the gorgeous picture of the popular imagination, sat the gilded chieftain on a throne of gold, surrounded by golden treasures of incomparable and boundless value.

In 1529, Alfinger set out from Coro with 200 men, and 1,000 slaves, loaded with provisions like pack mules. The methods of Cortes and Pizarro were mild and humane in comparison with his treatment of the natives. Slaughter and torture were both diversion and business in the extraction of gold. When about thirty thousand dollars' worth had been secured, fifty men with a hundred slaves were ordered to return with it to Coro. The dense forests, vine-entangled undergrowth, and insect-infested swamps, impeded their progress and one by one the slaves sank beneath their burdens of gold until the Spaniards found themselves the bearers of the precious cargo. Presently there were frequent accidents by which the golden loads were lost in the swamps, and by the end of a month there were neither slaves nor burdens and the fifty men had been reduced to less than a score by fever and famine. Three men, naked and dying, reached Coro. A year later, Alfinger returned with a ragged handful of his men and about two hundred slaves bearing about forty thousand dollars' worth of gold.

On April 5, 1536, when the whole of Spain was burning with the fever excited by the marvellous treasures of Peru, Georg von Speyer, the German Governor of Venezuela, gathered a force of about fifteen hundred men, determined to find El Dorado and his temples of untold gold. Half of this command was intrusted to the governor's lieutenant, a young licentiate, Gonzalo Ximenez de Quesada of Granada, who, from the extensiveness of his conquests, became known as El Conquistador. He was the Cortes and Pizarro of Northern South America without their excessive cruelty. Early in 1537 he reached the plains of Cundinamarca with 166 men, having lost nearly six hundred through hunger and hardship. Here was the home of El Dorado, such as it was outside of the myths.

According to Pedro Simon, the Jesuit historian of that time, and

ONE BY ONE THE SLAVES SANK BENEATH THEIR BURDENS OF GOLD.

another careful investigator, Piedrahita, Bishop of Panama, the gilded man ceased to exist two years before the discovery of America, but his fame continued among the natives all over South America. They told the story wherever they met Spaniards, whose excitable imaginations at once connected him with the lost treasures of the Incas. D'Acosta explained the legend as follows:

"When the chief of Guatavita was independent, he made a solemn sacrifice every year, which, for its singularity, contributed to give celebrity to the lake Guatavita. On the day appointed the chief smeared his body with turpentine, and then rolled in gold dust. Thus gilded and resplendent, he entered a canoe, surrounded by his nobles, whilst an immense multitude of people, with music and songs, crowded around the shores of the lake. Having reached the centre, the chief deposited his offerings of gold, emeralds, and other precious things, and then jumped in to bathe. At this moment the surrounding hills echoed with the applause of the people; and, when the religious ceremony concluded, the dancing, singing and drinking began."

In 1590, the Muysca Indians of Bogota made war on the tribe of the gilded man and almost destroyed them, thus putting an end to the ceremonies of El Dorado.

When the Spaniards suddenly appeared before the first village of the Muysca Indians on the plains of Cundinamarca, the natives fled in terror from what they believed to be man-eating monsters, and fortified themselves in a ravine near Zorocota. After trying in vain to dislodge them from their stronghold, Quesada returned discouraged to his camp. As the hungry Spaniards were eating the food they had captured, two horses broke loose and ran snorting and chasing each other toward the Indian warriors. Believing that the strange beasts had been let loose upon them to devour them, they fled to the highest points of the overhanging rocks.

At the ravine the Spaniards found an old man bound to a stake. A red cap was placed on his head and he was set free. Supposing that the man had been returned because he was considered too old for food, the natives cast several children over the rocks into the camp. As the Spaniards pityingly buried the unfortunate infants, the Indians then sent into camp by some slaves, two young women and a live stag. The strangers showed their appreciation by eating the stag and returning the women loaded with presents that appeared very costly to them. Thus reassured, the natives visited the Spanish camp and entered into a friendly alliance.

At Guatavita, the home of the Dorado, Quesada met the fiercest resistance. When they were at last conquered not an ounce of gold could be found. It was said that the inestimable treasures had been thrown into the lake. Some years later the lake was dragged to see if the lost treasures could be recovered, but the bottom was so soft and the water so deep that only a few insignificant ornaments could be found. In the lagoon of Siecha, a group of ten golden figures was recovered representing the gilded chieftain on a raft.

Quesada secured his first considerable treasure at the chief remaining village of the Tunja Indians, who had formerly been subjects of El Dorado. When the booty was heaped in the courtyard it made a pile so high that a horse and rider could be hidden behind it.

"Peru! Peru!" cried the delighted victors. "We have found a second Cassamalca and Cuzco."

The temple of Iraca promised a still greater amount, but while it was being despoiled the building caught fire and was consumed with all its great store of gold, silver, and emeralds. Notwithstanding all the losses, the treasure secured amounted to about three hundred thousand dollars in gold, half as much more in silver and at least a quarter million in emeralds.

Near the Spanish headquarters, Quesada founded, in 1538, the present city of Bogota, now the capital of the United States of Colombia. In 1540, a brother of the conqueror tried to drain Guatavita, the lake of El Dorado, but he succeeded only partially, recovering in all about five thousand dollars for his trouble.

But no one had yet seen the gilded chieftain and his countless treasures. The interest in him was therefore unabated and every story of captured treasures only heated the imagination of the fortune hunters and adventurers all the more.

In 1541 the Welsers sent Philip von Hutten, a knight of Wurtemburg, with a hundred horsemen along the trail of Quesada. They became lost and for two years wandered about the wilderness, at last coming back to the place where they had lost the trail. Having collected among the natives satisfactory evidence that the gold lands were to the east, he set out in that direction with forty horsemen. In a few days they came to fields cultivated by slaves and then to a bowl-shaped valley, in the centre of which was a town larger and more substantially built than any they had yet seen in South America. It was built regularly around a great public square, in which stood a temple towering high above the others. The smooth walls of yellow clay glistened in the declining sun and the excited imagination of both Spaniards and Germans saw before them the long-sought city of El Dorado. As they talked among themselves, they grew more and more sure that before them was a city built of gold in which there were greater spoils for the mere taking than had ever been seen in all the careers of Cortes and Pizarro.

Carefully adjusting their armour, and looking to their weapons, they fell into line and charged down the hill at full speed. What the natives thought when they beheld the apparition of flying steeds may not be known, but the war drums sounded and warriors swarmed into the streets and fearlessly met the frightful and unknown foe just outside the town. At the place of meeting the ground was cut with gullies and piled with rocks. The savages had the advantage and with the greatest difficulty Von Hutten succeeded in escaping to a battle-ground favourable to horsemen. Darkness had come on with the suddenness common to such latitudes and the Omaguas, as this famous tribe was called, left the field for the night. Fray Pedro Simon says that the next morning fifteen thousand or more Indians appeared ready for the battle.

Having in mind the valiant examples of the conquerors in Mexico and Peru, the horsemen charged compactly into the mass of savages. But the Omaguas were a different people. They fought with caution and courage. The confident onslaught was turned into a struggle for life. Nearly half of the men had been torn from their horses and slain before the remainder succeeded in cutting their way out of the host of warriors and escaping. The fame of the Omaguas spread and the whole gold-seeking world became convinced that their capital city was the home of the Dorado with all his fabulous treasures. It therefore became the object of many expeditions, but its distance from the coast and the fierceness of its warriors protected it successfully from European greed and invested it with all the colours of the wildest romance.

Two hundred years later, the Omaguas were visited by La Condamine, and he found a flourishing and home-loving people. Yet another hundred years and Lieutenant Herndon found them, in 1852, with the same virtues, but consisting all told of only 232 persons.

When the Spaniards of Peru heard the story of the golden capital of the Omaguas, it fitted so well the stories current among the Peruvians of the lost treasures of the Incas that the fever for conquest again seized the followers of Almagro and Pizarro, who had been so long

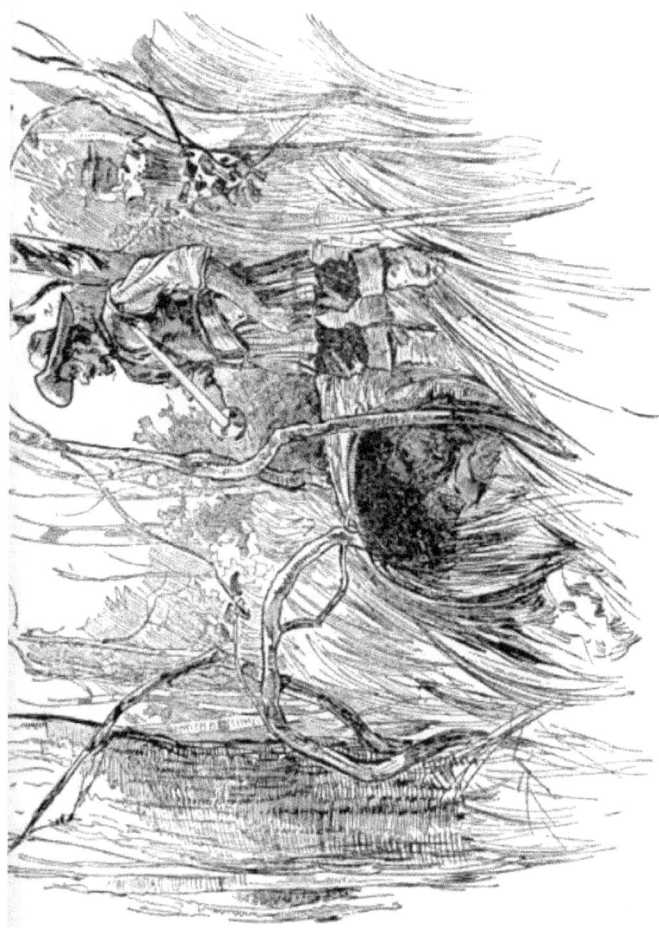

MALDONADO SAVED HIMSELF BY HIDING IN A HOLLOW LOG.

engaged chiefly in slaying each other in their bloody feuds.

In 1555, when the Marquis of Canete, a scion of the noble house of Mendoza, was appointed viceroy of Peru, he broke the destructive domestic conflict by sending the leaders away on adventurous expeditions in search of the Dorado and the golden capital of the Omaguas. It was the universal testimony of the Peruvians that after the capture of the Inca Atahuallpa at Cassamalca by Pizarro, forty thousand of the nobility assembled vast stores of their most precious and costly treasures, which they carried across the Andes east of Cuzco, where they founded a golden city in the midst of the great forests, inaccessible to horsemen.

Juan Alvarez Maldonado, one of the most turbulent of the Almagro faction, was given the special task to discover and despoil that city. Gomez de Tordoya, one of the partisans of the Pizarros, heard of this and hastily fitted out a rival expedition, intending to get to the scene of the spoils before Maldonado. There was a rush between the two packs of Spanish wolves to see which could first reach the golden spoils. Tordoya reached the shores of the Tono River first, but was soon overtaken by Maldonado. They fell upon one another and fought for three days, when, with nearly half killed on each side, Tordoya's men surrendered. Meantime great numbers of the Chunchos Indians had been gathering and they watched the singular conflict with unabated delight. At its conclusion, they fell upon the exhausted survivors and killed all but Maldonado, who saved himself by hiding in a hollow log. He was an enormously fat man, but his energy and endurance was such that he succeeded in escaping back across the Andes to Cuzco.

Where gold was the lure, no disaster was sufficient to dampen the ardour and enthusiasm of the Spaniard. Pedro Hernandez de Serpa landed at Cuma with one of the largest forces that had ever sought to penetrate to the golden city, but not a man ever returned from the great forests which they entered with boundless enthusiasm. In March, 1570, Don Pedro de Silvia left Burburuta with the purpose of finding the Dorado. He crossed the Llonos and arrived in Peru with less than a fourth of his men, and still the fame of the spoils of El Dorado and the golden capital of the Omaguas increased with every failure. Gonzalo Pizarro, brother of the great conqueror, sought to retrieve his falling fortunes by crossing the Andes in search of El Dorado, and all the great geographers of that time gave a definite location to the mythical city of Manoa on the mythical great White Sea. Even as late as 1844 Van Heuvel, a native of New York City, travelling in Guiana, wrote a book in the full belief that there was a veritable Dorado living in the golden city of Manoa on the Mar Blanco.

For three centuries the whole of South America was filled with the most wonderful stories of these golden places and the most remarkable experiences and adventures were continually occurring in the fruitless searches for them.

Don Enrique Rubio was one of the first to claim the glory of having seen the Dorado in his temple in the singular city of Manoa on the Mar Blanco. On one of the expeditions, three Omagua chiefs were treacherously taken prisoners at a council to which they had been invited. On the following day they were to be tortured to death, as many hundreds of Indians had been before them, with the purpose of forcing them to reveal the location of their golden city. Rubio conceived the idea of playing a role for his own profit and glory. He made himself appear to be the friend of the chiefs, that he greatly deplored the treachery that had been practiced upon them, and that he would liberate them if he could find the opportunity. He possessed sufficient knowledge of the Indian languages to make himself understood, and by shielding them from indignities he gained their confidence. When morning came it was discovered that Rubio and the three chiefs had disappeared. A year passed and Rubio returned to Cuzco with a story of having visited El Dorado, which was the basis for many of the remarkable romances that spread over Spanish America.

In 1531, Diego de Ordas was sent eastward on an expedition in search of El Dorado and he got as far as the mouth of the Caroni on the Orinoco, when all his powder was destroyed while being dried in the sun. This was said to have been caused by the negligence of Juan Martinez, the munitioneer. He was accordingly tried and sentenced to death, but the intercession of his comrades caused Ordas to alter the punishment to that of being placed in a canoe without oars or food and set adrift in the Orinoco.

Nearly two years later some Indians brought a white man to the Island of Margarita, who was wasted almost to a skeleton by starvation, naked, except for untanned skins tied about his feet and loins, and so crazed that he did not know his name. A ship was about to leave for Porto Rico and the captain carried the unfortunate man to San Juan, where he was cared for in a convent of Dominican friars. He talked incessantly, though incoherently, of the golden shores of the Mar Blanco, and of the golden temples of Manoa. Although his wasted system could not recuperate, his mind was restored to health under the attentive care of the fathers. So far he had never allowed the skin that was bound about his loins to be touched by any one. He now took it off and gave it to the friars, who found that it contained several pounds of gold that looked like very coarse sand. On being questioned, he told a remarkable story of the experience that had brought him to such a state.

He was Juan Martinez, who had been set adrift by Diego de Ordas. The terror of the awful solitudes had been harder to bear than his suffering for food. The monsters of the swamps had followed him by day and the fierce animals of the dark woods had tried to make him their prey at night. In this state he took a fever and lay down in the bottom of his boat to die. How long he floated that way he could not tell, for he first came to consciousness by hearing voices of men near him. They touched him and spoke to him as with great curiosity, since he was the first white man they had ever seen. When he tried to walk and could not they carried him with great tenderness upon their backs. Presently they blindfolded him and carried him thus fourteen days. At last he heard many voices about him from men, women, and children. The blindfold was taken off and he saw around him the houses of a great city.

Over the portals of every door were images of gold, and soon they came to a clear lake more than a league across, around whose shores he could see temples and palaces supported on rows of great golden pillars. Seeing the remarkable brilliancy of the sand along the shore, he asked to be set down a moment, when he scooped up a handful and found to his amazement that it was all pure gold.

The following morning he was taken before the king, who sat on a massive throne in the temple of the sun, attended by a hundred virgins. The stranger was treated very kindly and was adopted into the nation through a curious ceremony of immersion in a great basin of perfumed water, followed by sprinkling with a dust of gold and then another immersion in the lake. Everybody then treated him as a brother and he soon recovered and grew strong. He remained seven months, and never in all that time saw an act of crime or a single case of distress that it was possible to relieve, for every one believed that the well-being of every other person was of equal importance with his own, and friendship was the only law.

However, there came a time when he began to long to see people of his own customs, habit, and religion. He asked consent to be allowed to go on to the rising sun where his people lived, and permission was readily given. Half a dozen warriors were appointed to conduct him to the borders of the kingdom, and as he passed by the shores of the Mar Blanco he filled several small bags with the sands of gold and tied them about his waist.

As he was about to part from his friends at the border they were suddenly set upon by a party of hunters and killed. Martinez succeeded in hiding himself in some driftwood, and so escaped, but the horrors of the forest became even greater than before, and he lost all memory of his experiences until he found himself being cared for at the island of Margarita off the mouth of the Orinoco.

The good Dominican fathers of San Juan took down in detail the elaborate testimony of the dying man and sent the gold sand to the King of Spain. It was one of the sensations of Europe, rivalling in public interest the discoveries and conquests of Cortes, Pizarro, and Quesada. Geographers placed the city of Manoa and Mar Blanco on their maps, and historians discussed very learnedly in their writings, the probable location of the city of gold and the lake of priceless sands. England, Portugal, and Holland vied with Spain in expeditions sent out by their respective governments in search for the wonderful home of El Dorado, but the city of the unfortunate Juan Martinez was never found.

Among the extraordinary adventures occasioned by the search for El Dorado one of the strangest was that of two priests and six soldiers in 1640. A soldier came privately to the Governor at Moyobamba, claiming that he had seen the golden city. He was the only survivor of a score of men who had set out alone to find the home of the gilded chief from directions given by a friendly Indian. The others had all perished from the hardships of the journey.

The governor sent two hundred men, under his guidance, to verify his discoveries. After two weeks' travel nearly due eastward to one of the tributaries of the Maranon, the guide insisted that it was necessary for the gilded chieftain to be first approached by an embassy consisting of a dozen men and two priests. It would take them only four days to make this reconnoissance and return. Accordingly the two priests and twelve men set forth to open friendly negotiations with El Dorado. The army waited in vain for their return. Scouting parties were sent out, but neither Spaniards nor signs of inhabitants could be found, much less of the far-famed golden city.

Late in the following year, the two priests and six of the soldiers arrived at Para on the mouth of the Amazon, all of them maniacs, who never recovered their reason. They raved incessantly till their death about the golden sands of Lake Parima and the horrible tortures that had been inflicted upon them in the temple of the sun. Their story created great excitement in Brazil and led to many fruitless expeditions.

Of all the marvellous adventures through the vast wildernesses of the Amazon, from the voyage of Orellana in 1540, none equalled in heroism the last that is worthy of special mention. This journey, in 1769, was not that of a lot of sinewy and hardened men, but by a delicate and refined woman, doubtless the greatest feat ever performed by a woman. Many historians concede to her the honour of being the greatest heroine known in the history of South America.

Her story is told in full by her husband in a letter to the historian La Condamine, which was published in that writer's book of Journeys through South America.

Her husband had been absent several years on a scientific expedition for the government, intended to clear up many myths, when she heard that he had arrived at a certain point on one of the tributaries of the Amazon and was preparing to send for her. Wishing in her fondness and joy to anticipate him, she set forth to meet him with her two brothers, two maids, and three male servants. With amazing perseverance and resolution, she continued on and on until the point was reached where her husband was said to be, only to find that it was all false. He had never been near there. By this time their horses were dead, and to attempt to return by foot through the difficulties they had encountered was certain death. Near them was the Amazon, at whose mouth they knew there were Christian settlements. It was their only hope. They got a boat from some friendly Indians and set themselves adrift on the stream that was to carry them through the awful tunnel of forests to the distant sea.

After a time their boat was destroyed in some rapids and they continued on foot through the noxious jungles. One by one the two maids and five men died, until she was alone, but undaunted she continued on. After seven months she reached the territory of some Indians who were friendly to the French settlements about ten days' journey away. There they carried her, where she was kindly cared for until her wasted and famine-stricken body was restored, but her snow-white hair remained as a witness to her unparalleled suffering and courage.

Her husband supposed she had perished, but a few years later she was able to communicate to him her safety and there was a happy meeting in Venezuela after a separation of fourteen years.

Adventures of the Maranones

It is remarkable that the first declaration of independence in America was issued by the craziest lot of brigands ever known. It was a formal document drawn up and signed by the Maranones on the Amazon and forwarded to King Philip of Spain in the year 1561. Whether the leader was a maniac or a monster he may be safely granted the palm of being the most detestable character produced in the conquest of America, and of having conducted the wildest and most appalling expedition in the annals of history.

In 1548, two hundred soldiers filed out of the public square of Potosi on their way to Tucuman. Although it was against the law, each soldier had an Indian slave to carry his baggage. The licentiate of the town, not having the means at hand to enforce the law against so many, and yet not wishing to see it utterly ignored, seized the last man passing the gate and ordered him to be given the full penalty of two hundred lashes. This soldier, known as Lope de Aguirre, implored the licentiate or *alcalde* to put him to death rather than to have him flogged, since he was a gentleman by birth and the brother of a man who was lord of vassals in Spain.

But the *alcalde* decided that an example must be made and ordered the punishment to be given regardless of petitions from both citizens and soldiers. Accordingly, the accused was stripped naked and put astride backwards on a donkey. In this state, he was publicly whipped at the crossings of all the streets in the town.

Aguirre refused to proceed on his way to Tecuman, but remained at Potosi. Esquivel, the licentiate *alcalde*, divining that revenge was meditated, surrounded himself with a strong guard, and when his term of office expired, removed to Lima. Aguirre followed him, openly asserting that nothing but the death of the licentiate by assassination would avenge the insult of the punishment that had been given.

Esquivel removed secretly to Quito, then to Cuzco, but Aguirre followed him with the persistence and menace of a bloodhound, going all the way from place to place on foot, without shoes or decent clothing, saying that a gentleman so disgraced as himself had no right to live among civilized people, or to avail himself of the conveniences of Christians until the shame had been blotted out in blood.

Esquivel went heavily armed day and night, accompanied by a servant likewise prepared. The judge at Cuzco ordered the officers of the peace to keep a strict watch for the arrival of Aguirre and to arrest him at the first suspicious act.

For three years and four months the implacable Spaniard pursued the purpose of revenge without an opportunity for its execution. When Aguirre found that Esquivel was at Cuzco, he determined to wait no longer for opportunities. On a certain Monday at noon, the singular avenger reached Cuzco, inquired for the house of Esquivel, and having found it, boldly entered. Stabbing the watchman or bodyguard before an outcry could be raised, he searched through the rooms until he found the lawyer at work in his library. There he informed the surprised enemy in measured terms that one of them must die within the hour in honourable duel with swords. No alternative was at hand, and when some visitors came in later in the day they found the lawyer face downward upon the floor grasping a broken sword in his lifeless hand.

Aguirre sought out a brother of one of his comrades in the army who successfully concealed the murderer through nearly two months of vigilant search, when, disguised as a negro, he got safely out of the country.

About this time, two hundred Indians arrived at La Fronteria in Peru with the remarkable story that they had started four thousand strong from the mouth of the Amazon River, led by two Portuguese, in search of El Dorado. All the rest had perished. The land of the Dorado had been found when they were too weak and disorganized to attempt any conquest. Their testimony corroborated the wildest fiction known of the inexhaustible treasures awaiting the spoilsmen in the golden city of the Omaguas.

Anarchy had heretofore reigned in Peru, but at this time Hurtado de Mendoza, Marquis of Caneta, was enforcing the law and bringing order out of chaos. In consequence there was an ungovernable rabble of ruffians who were anxious to leave the country and whom the viceroy was as anxious to see depart.

THEY FOUND THE LAWYER FACE DOWNWARD UPON THE FLOOR, GRASPING A
BROKEN SWORD.

The story of the Brazilian Indians afforded the desired opportunity to the governor. He organized an expedition to overrun the territory of the Omaguas and to capture their golden city and gilded chieftain. As was expected, all the outlaws and malefactors of the country flocked to the standard of the expedition. A strong man was needed to lead such an army, and the viceroy selected Pedro de Ursua, a knight who was related to the overseer of Ximines de Quesada, conqueror of Cundinamarca.

The army of about a thousand men, and as many slaves, was accompanied by a large number of colonists with their household goods, who were to form the proposed settlements in the land of the Dorado. In this way there were included about a hundred women. Ursua, the leader, was devoted to Inez de Atienza of Pinira, the young and beautiful widow of Pedro de Arcos. Castellanos, who received his information from survivors of the marvellous expedition, bears testimony to her beauty, accomplishments, and spirited youth. He believed her to have been an honourable and virtuous woman. Vasquez, who was with the expedition, and Ortiguera, who had access to reliable information, both assert that she was the mistress of Ursua, and Vasquez lays to her charge the murder of that unfortunate captain, but the writings of those men convict them of the inclination to blacken a woman's character rather than to defend it. Simon and Piedrahita, two friars who regarded women as the special instruments of Satan, and who got their facts sixty-two years later, spare no terms in heaping abuse upon her.

Others, however, regard her as one of the greatest heroines of Spanish America, as well as one having the most pitiful career. This much seems true that when Pedro de Ursua, the chivalrous knight of Navarre, already famous in Peru for his subjugation of the savages about Quito, met the beautiful and accomplished Doña Inez, they fell deeply in love with each other. Then he was sent on a long and dangerous mission across the Cordilleras from which it was likely that he would never return. The gently nurtured woman abandoned the luxuries and comforts of an elegant home, against the remonstrances of her friends, to brave the unknown dangers of a search for El Dorado in an expedition with her lover. Simon pauses in the midst of his vituperation of her character to admit that before the departure of the expedition, Ursua took the Lady Inez with him to Moyombamba with the expressed intention of marrying her, and there is not a word of evidence from any source that this was not done. Simon asserts that after the death of Ursua she displayed the utmost vileness in becoming the mistress of his murderers, but it may be remembered in her favour that she was a helpless and broken-hearted woman in the power of the most abandoned ruffians known among the maleactors of Spanish America.

In July, 1560, the army and colonists started across the Andes upon their mad and murderous cruise down the Amazon and through two thousand miles of almost uninhabitable forests. Such were their difficulties in travel that in a few weeks three hundred horses, six hundred cattle, and nearly all the household goods were abandoned. At the end of six months, most of the colonists, being unused to such hardships, had died, and there was general discontent in the army. The occasion was ripe for a conspiracy and the conspirator was at hand.

Ursua decided to stop at a point known as Machiparo to rest and repair their boats. This was the opportunity desired by the arch malefactor, Lope de Aguirre. From the day when he had been publicly flogged through the streets of Potosi, he had day and night meditated revenge against the state whose laws were the cause of his disgrace. The long sought means seemed now at hand, and with consummate cunning and address he took advantage of the opportunity. He gathered together the malcontents and proposed to remove Ursua and place their own men at the head.

On New Year's night, while Juan Gomez was sentinel before the captain's tent, a figure clothed as a ghost, passed by exclaiming, "Pedro de Ursua, knight of Navarre and Governor of Omagua and El Dorado, may God have mercy on thy soul."

The captain called to the sentinel to know who had spoken and what had been said. The trembling sentinel told him, but he made light of the warning and returned to sleep. The next evening, two hours after sunset, some of the conspirators came up to him where he lay in his hammock, and before he could defend himself, ran him through with their swords.

Aguirre showed the mutineers that through this act they had become outlaws without hope of mercy from Spain. He urged them to return to Peru and effect the independence of that country, but the larger faction, under Fernando de Guzman, decided to continue in pursuit of El Dorado. At the mouth of the Japura River, a three months' rest took place, during which Aguirre attained complete ascendancy in the councils of the army. Assassination was the order of both day and night, and a word uttered against the will of the leader meant death. His ambition broadened into a scheme of unparalleled audacity. Strong brigantines were built, in which they were to sail down the river to the sea, capture the island of Margarita, take by surprise Nombre de Dios and Panama, and from these vantage points effect the liberation of Spanish America. Accordingly a declaration of independence, the first issued in America, was drawn up, and signed by every member of the army excepting three, one of whom, Francisco Vasquez, succeeded in preserving his life, and afterward became the historian of the expedition.

The declaration was a remarkable document addressed to "King Philip, native of Spain, son of Charles the Invincible," and ran as follows:

I, Lope de Aguirre, thy vassal, a Christian of poor, but noble parents, and native of the town of Onate in Biscay, went over-young to Peru to labour, lance in hand. I fought for thy glory; but I recommend to thee to be more just to the good vassals whom thou hast in this country. I and mine, weary of the cruelties and injustice which thy viceroy, thy governors, and thy judges exercise in thy name, have resolved to obey thee no more.

We regard ourselves no longer as Spaniards. We make relentless war on thee because we will no longer endure the oppression of thy ministers. We care no more for thy pardon or thy wrath than for the books of Martin Luther.

The conquest of this country has been without danger or cost to thee, and thou hast no more right than I to draw revenues from these provinces, or to oppress the people for being listless to thy will.

After reaching Venezuela, Aguirre liberated a captive monk on his oath that he would carry this delectable document to the king.

So indistinct was the geography of that time that no one knows whether they sailed on down the Amazon or went through one of the numerous connecting *bayous* into the Orinoco. In either case it was at this point in the amazing expedition where the brutal mastery of Aguirre became unassailable. His tyranny was so terrible that those who hated him most were his most servile tools. To gain his favour they committed crimes so sickening and revolting as to present a unique phenomenon in human nature.

There was one exception. In that awful time Doña Inez became the sole counsellor and guardian of the score or more of women yet living. To save them alive until civilization could be reached was her appalling task. If it is true that virtue was traded for life, it only accentuates the execration due to the monsters in power, and in no way excuses the historians who delight to blacken the character of Doña Inez. That Aguirre hated and feared her is testimony enough to her heroism, however questionable may have been her judgment of the means necessary to avert death to her and the defenceless women who looked to her for help in those days of paralyzing terror.

At last every known enemy of Aguirre had fallen and he dared to order her assassination. Llamaso and Carrion, two candidates for the favour of the leader, entered her tent, and in the midst of the screams of her companions, killed her in the most revolting manner. Of this foul deed, Castellanos poetically wrote:

The birds mourned on the trees, the wild beasts of the forests lamented, the waters in the rivulets ceased to sing on their way through the flowers, and the winds uttered their execrations over the horrid crime, as Llamaso and Carrion severed the veins of her white throat. Wretches! Wert thou born of woman? No! for even the beasts could not bring forth a man so vile. How didst thou survive the imagination of so enormous a wrong? Only that thy minds were dead and thy souls were fled from such foul clay.

None dared to touch her body excepting her two devoted servants, who buried her at the foot of an evergreen tree and covered her grave with the wild flowers that grew around. On the bark of the tree they cut these words. "Here lies one whose faithfulness and beauty were unequalled and whom cruel men slew without cause."

After this the brutalities to the women were such that many of them committed suicide. Only two received protection. These were the young half-breed daughter of Aguirre and her companion, Doña Torralva.

The horrors of their deeds were fully matched by the fantastic follies committed. Fernando de Guzman of Seville, with many ridiculous ceremonies, was made "Prince and King of Tierra Firma and of Peru." He insisted on the court etiquette due a king, and thus produced the dissatisfaction that gave an excuse to Aguirre for the puppet king's assassination.

The next morning after Guzman's death, Aguirre surrounded

131

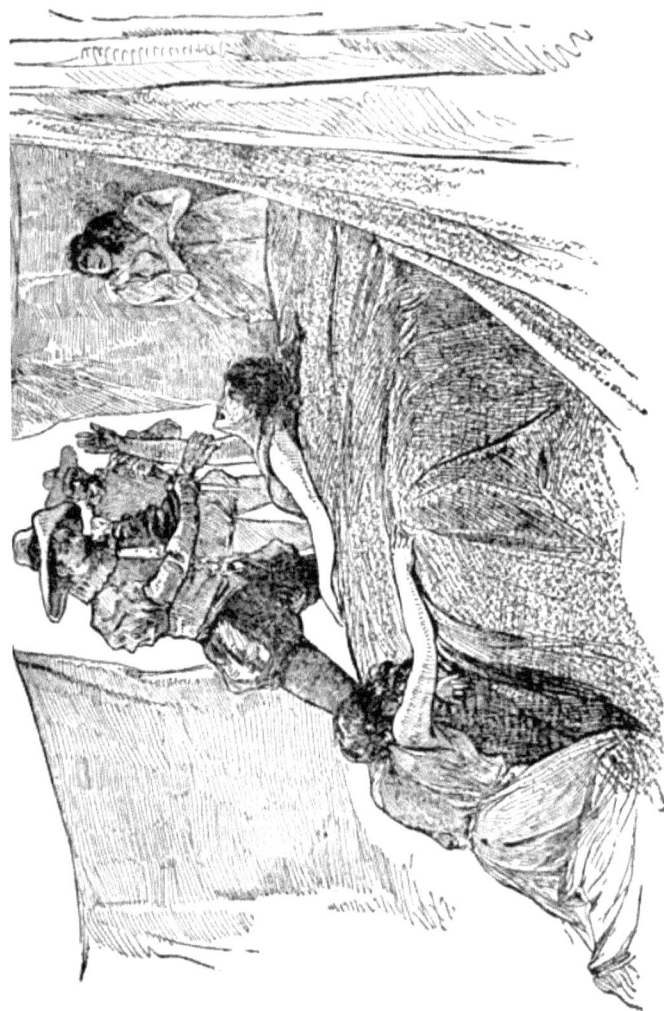

LLAMASO AND CARRION KILLED HER IN THE MOST REVOLTING MANNER.

himself with eighty of his special retainers and proclaimed himself "General of the Maranon." Henceforth his army was known as the Maranones. This name was in use at that time among some geographers and historians for the river now known as the Amazon, but there is much reason to think that the Maranones were then on the Orinoco.

About the middle of July, 1561, the *brigantines* carrying the Maranones, now reduced to less than two hundred men, reached the island of Margarita. Their arrival created great curiosity and general astonishment. The governor, *alcalde* and their official companions decided to pay a visit of welcome to the strange wanderers. Aguirre waylaid his visitors and took them all prisoners. He then marched on to the town, took the fort by surprise and possessed himself of the island without opposition. All provisions, merchandise and money to be found were divided among his soldiers. The protesting citizens were imprisoned or slain, and the women were given up without mercy to the debauchery of the ruthless ruffians. No pirates or buccaneers at a later day ever more brutally ravaged a Spanish settlement than did these savage followers of Aguirre.

He needed for further conquest a stronger vessel than his *brigantines*, and seeing such a ship anchored at Piritu, near the mainland opposite to Margarita, he sent some Maranones to seize it. They took the opportunity to desert, and when the vessel approached Margarita it was flying the royal flag. In the meantime, Aguirre was so sure of the vessel that he had sunk his *brigantines*. When he saw the ship nearing the harbour under the colours of Spain, he placed all the officers and the principal citizens in the fort and ordered them to be strangled at midnight. This was done with the usual promptitude. He then set the bodies upright in an orderly row and called all his soldiers together in a kind of "parade rest" and made them a speech.

> Well do you see, O Maranones, in the bodies before your eyes that, independent of the crimes you committed in the River Maranon, you have divested yourselves of all rights in the Kingdom of Castile, You have foresworn allegiance to the king by swearing to make perpetual war upon him, and you have signed your names to the act. After adding yet many crimes, you executed your sworn prince and lord, many captains and soldiers, a priest and a noble lady. Having arrived at this island you have forcibly taken possession of it, divided the property found in it

among yourselves, and committed sundry and divers wickedness. Now you have killed another governor, an *alcalde*, a *regidor*, an *alguazil* mayor, and certain other citizens whose bodies are now witnesses before you.

Be not deceived by any vain confidence; for, having committed so many and such abominable and atrocious crimes, be ye sure that ye are not safe in any part of the world, excepting with me. Suppose that by some chance you should achieve the king's pardon, know this, that the friends and kindred of the dead would follow you until vengeance was done.

"Thus are you gravely warned to be united with me, for therein lies the question of life and death.

The following day the vessel bearing the deserters sailed away to warn the coast and to provide means for the capture of the traitor. Aguirre was furious and he began to suspect even his most servile companions. Martin Perez had long been a faithful officer as master of the camp, but someone anxious to appear zealous in devotion to Aguirre told him that Perez seemed to be acting suspiciously. The assassination of the master of the camp was ordered, but the sickening butchery was done in such a bungling manner that he lay still alive on the floor, brained and mutilated beyond recognition when Aguirre came in. While he was looking at the writhing body, Anton Llamoso, who among other crimes had done the heinous murder of Doña Inez, chanced to walk in. Someone whispered to Aguirre, "There is a friend of Perez."

"They tell me that you are a friend to this traitor," he said, turning to the astonished Llamoso. "How is this? Do you call that friendship to me? And do you hold thus lightly the love I feel for you?"

As a study in the debasement of men, the scene that followed is given in the language of Fray Pedro Simon, from his *Sixth Historical Notice of the Conquest of Tierra Firma*.

Those who had slain Martin Perez, and who were then dripping with his blood, being desirous to do more murder, had scarcely heard Aguirre's words to Llamoso, when they gathered close around eager for the signal to slay him.

The great fear that at once fell upon the wretch, made him haste with violent protestations, backing them up by many horrible oaths, mixed with vehement blasphemies against those who accused him, saying that such treason to his lord had never entered his thoughts, and that Aguirre ought to believe him for the faithfulness and affection which he had always been happy to show.

Aguirre did not speak at once and it seemed to Llamoso that the brutal master was not satisfied with the servile words, so he rushed upon the body of Martin Perez, almost cut to pieces, yet moving with departing life, and threw himself with madness upon it, shouting with desperate frenzy, 'Cursed be this abominable traitor who meditated so foul a crime against my beloved lord. I will drink his blood and eat his brain.'

So saying, the abandoned wretch in frantic terror put his mouth to the crushed head, with more than demoniac rage, and applied himself with the appalling acts of a famished beast. Rising he stood trembling before Aguirre with the bloody visage of a demon, awaiting the returning confidence of his master.

'It is well,' said that monster. 'He is faithful.'

In a transport of joy Llamoso embraced him and they went out arm in arm. And thus it at last came about that he was indeed faithful, for there was no one who sustained Aguirre until his last hour like unto this same Llamoso.

The startling news given by the deserters spread over the coast and the alarmed governments of Santo Domingo, Santa Martha, Merida, and Cartagena made hasty preparations to defend themselves and to capture the monster whose hideousness grew with every account.

Three small fishing smacks opportunely arrived at this time in the bay of Margarita and were seized by Aguirre. On the last Sunday in August, 1561, having destroyed nearly all the property and people of the island, during the forty days' sojourn, Aguirre and his men left for the mainland. A storm drove them to Burburata. The Governor of Venezuela immediately called out all his available forces to capture the remarkable band of unparalleled fiends.

The Maranones arrived in the harbour about nightfall. To guard themselves from a night attack, they run ashore their own vessels and those in the harbour and set them on fire. In the circle of bright light they slept unmolested on the beach. In the morning they went into the town, but found it deserted. Then, in a style that would have been the admiration and envy of the buccaneers and pirates who ravaged the same coast in after years, they ranged over the surrounding country and terrorized the inhabitants.

IN THE MORNING THEY WENT INTO THE TOWN BUT FOUND IT DESERTED.

When Pedro Nunez, the principal merchant of Venezuela, was captured and brought to Aguirre, the chief asked him why the people had fled.

"Most certainly because of fear," was the reply.

"But what do you yourself think of me and my men?" persisted Aguirre.

Believing a pretext was sought for killing him, the tradesman did not answer.

"Give your opinion freely, and fear not for yourself," insisted Aguirre with a great show of candour, "we are your friends."

Being thus pressed for an answer, the unfortunate tradesman ventured to say that he greatly feared that they were Lutherans.

"Stupid barbarian!" cried the chief, horror-stricken and enraged at the charge. "Is it possible that thou art such an ignorant savage as to conceive such a horrid calumny? I do not now dash thee to earth with my helmet, only that at a more fitting season I may chastise thee with a death becoming to thy impious traducement."

On the next day the army was drawn up to see strangled the wretched man who had so foully slandered them.

It was at this place where Aguirre permitted Father Pedro Contreras to return to his charge at the desolate island of Margarita, on the priest's oath that he would carry to the King of Spain the declaration of independence drawn up by the Maranones in the wilderness of the Amazon.

Advancing on through Valencia, he laid waste the country and continued to commit the most unspeakable atrocities on to Barquicimeto, where the king's forces were collecting. In the march through the wilderness, many found opportunities to desert, and a proclamation of pardon to deserters caused the army of the Maranones to diminish rapidly.

Garcia de Paredes, having charge of the royal force, marched rapidly to the point where Aguirre had intrenched himself. As the king's troops appeared, the Maranones threw down their arms and ran to them crying, "Long live the King."

Only one man remained in the trenches with Aguirre. It was the pitiable wretch Anton Llamoso, who had killed Doña Inez, now exhibiting a less abhorrent evidence of fidelity.

Seeing the hopeless situation, Aguirre went to the tent of his daughter and her companion, Doña Torralva, all that remained alive of the hundred or more women who started with the expedition of conquerors and colonists. "My daughter, commend thyself to thy God," he said, "for I have come to kill thee, that thou mayst not be pointed at with scorn, nor be in the power of those who may call thee the daughter of a traitor."

Doña Torralva, not yet sixteen years of age, caught the *arquebuse* from his hands, but he thrust her aside and killed his daughter with his sword.

Just as he finished this dreadful work, the troops came up. The captain wanted to spare him for trial and public execution, but the Maranones demanded that he be killed at once. The captain consented and two Maranones fired their *arquebuses* at him, but not bringing him to the ground.

"Maranones!" he exclaimed, steadying himself against the pole of the tent, "you have aimed better before this. Try again."

They fired again.

"That is better," he managed to say, and fell dead.

The chief officer now coming up, ordered the murdered daughter to be buried in the churchyard of Barquicimeto, but the body of the infamous man was divided and distributed among the towns as a warning of the fate of traitors to the king. His head was placed in an iron cage and fastened over the door of the house of justice in Tocuyo.

Llamoso was taken to Pampluna, the town founded by Pedro de Ursua, the murdered commander of the expedition, and was there, as if in poetic justice, put to the garrotte and his body publicly burned.

It is said that the bloody prophesy of Aguirre came true. The Maranones carried the mark of Cain. All died the violent death of rabid malefactors. There was no place where they could hide from the vengeance of man and the law.

The natives of Venezuela believe that Aguirre still appears now and then among them as their evil spirit. Those who are benighted on the marshy plains tremble at unknown sounds, and, pointing to the strange swamp lights, cross themselves as they say, "It is the soul of Aguirre the traitor."

The Liberators

The problem that the United States has found in the government of Cuba, Porto Rico, and the Philippines, presents numerous curious phases of popular interest. The contrasts between the heroism of the liberators and the bloody anarchy that invariably followed freedom in every Spanish-American republic, furnish a subject for thoughtful speculation. Self-government, as understood by Abraham Lincoln, has not been even approximately approached by them through four generations. All their advancement has been made under the martial hand of wise dictators.

One of the dictator presidents of Venezuela, in a message to his congress, congratulated the country on the fact that there had been only seventeen revolutions during the past two years. Notwithstanding such a spectacle of hate, distrust, espionage, intrigue, immorality, assassination and anarchy, as everywhere prevailed, Spanish-America has produced many of the bravest and noblest men, and in its progress puts to shame the mother country, with all her advantages of European civilization.

The victory of Nelson in Trafalgar Bay, early in 1805, provided a favourable opportunity for the Spanish colonies to free themselves, and the usurpation of the throne of Spain by Joseph Bonaparte gave a political and religious excuse that appealed strongly to the popular mind.

A most exciting and adventurous period followed. The land of romance was again in a ferment. Once more there were men in the saddle anxious to rival the deeds of their steel-cased ancestors who followed the fortunes of the first conquerors.

Continuously from the time of the independence of the United States from England to the acknowledged independence of the Spanish colonies from Spain, the United States had ample reason for interference and equal opportunity to add Spanish territory. A study of comparative history shows that the United States has from first to last profited with extraordinary reluctance by the incompetency and cruelty of Spain. The beginning affords a peculiar example and an interesting parallel.

In 1805, a well-dressed and distinguished-looking foreigner came to New York from England and lodged at Mrs. Avery's boarding house in State street. To his fellow boarders he became known as George Martin. In a few days he received a letter from Washington City which caused him to take a hasty departure. As soon as the primitive methods of travel permitted, he reached the National capitol and was admitted to a private interview with President Jefferson and his Secretary of State, James Madison. At the hotel in Washington he was registered as Señor Molini. February 2nd, he returned to New York and at once went aboard the *Leander*, a merchant ship belonging to Samuel G. Ogden.

The *Leander* came to anchor between Staten Island and the Jersey shore. Two or three days later a Spanish gentleman suddenly appeared before the naval officer of the port with the charge that large quantities of arms and ammunition were being taken secretly on board that vessel at night. The officer turned to his books and found that the *Leander* was cleared for Jacquemel. Therefore there appeared to be no legal reason for interfering. But exciting rumours were at once set afloat as to the destination and object of the *Leander*.

Marquis Yrujo, of Spain, assisted by the French ambassador, lodged formal complaint with the government and through the *Philadelphia Gazette* accused Jefferson and Madison of criminal connivance with the enemies of Spain for the overthrow of Spanish power in America.

The Federal authorities arrested Mr. Ogden, owner of the Leander, and Colonel William Smith, son-in-law of John Adams, and the collector of the port of New York, each of whom were put under $20,000 bonds.

Political and personal accusations and recriminations waxed hot and burning epithets were hurled back and forth like fiery hand-grenades in a fight with pirates. Strange to say the dispute raged chiefly around the question as to whether the Federalists or the Democrats had the honour of being the best friends of the Spaniards. It was necessary to love the Spaniard in order to satisfy the popular hate for England. Meantime the Leander sailed away on its mission of liberation, the beginning that was to find an end ninety-three years later. But the opportune time was not yet at hand. The expedition was unsuccessful and the organizer with difficulty succeeded in escaping to England from Trinidad.

This adventurer had passed through a campaign with Washington nearly twenty years before, greatly honoured as Don Francisco de Miranda of Caracas. He fought with great credit through the Belgian campaign of 1793 with Dumouriez, and later became a favourite at the courts of both England and Russia. He did not cease his efforts with the failure of the *Leander* expedition, but devoted himself assiduously to the object of Spanish-American liberty. July 30, 1812, after another unsuccessful attempt at revolution, he was arrested at Laguira and delivered to the Spaniards, by Simon Bolivar, his subordinate companion in arms, who had signed the treaty of Victoria, five days before, restoring Venezuela to Spain. Miranda was imprisoned at San Carlos. After several months, he was sent to Porto Rico and then to Cadiz in Spain, where he perished some years later a prisoner in the dungeons of Fort La Caraca. It is recorded that when Bolivar, who is known as the Washington of South America, delivered his elder companion in arms to the Spanish authorities, he said, "I surrender Miranda in order to punish a traitor to my country, and not to do a service to the king."

It is true that the liberation of the greater part of South America was afterward effected under the leadership of Bolivar, and yet one of his lieutenants wrote a book to prove him a monster of tyranny, while there was constant rebellion against his authority and unceasing revolution under his government.

The deeds and achievements of the patriotic troops under Bolivar and his lieutenants equalled many of the heroic acts of the conquerors and rivalled the most thrilling records of patriotism in any country, but the moment the hand of the dictator was off of them there was immediate anarchy.

When the patriot army crossed the Andes to Santander, it had equalled the feat of Hannibal crossing the Alps. The bands that waded the perpetual swamps through the terrors of the tropical forests, were as devoted and courageous as those of Marion, Sumpter, Pickens, and Lee. The scene of Bolivar's wild and haggard band driving before them with unsparing slaughter the atrocious Barriera is more inspiring than that of Washington inactive at Valley Forge.

The Spanish foe was immeasurably more savage than Tyron or

AT PARTING HE PLACED A RING UPON HER FINGER.

Arnold in New England. Ferdinand VII of Spain ordered a war of extermination, and General Boves sacked the towns in his course of subjugation through Venezuela, not allowing the dead to be buried, but commanding that the bodies of men, women, and children be left rotting where they fell.

When Aragua was entered by Suasola, with about five hundred troops from the army of Monteverde, the inhabitants, numbering fifteen hundred, made a great public feast for them. After a merry hour, the soldiers, under secret orders, turned upon their entertainers and cut off the ears of every person in the town. A trunk full of these gruesome relics was sent to Monteverde's a proof of his lieutenant's fidelity and they were worn as souvenirs in the hatbands of the soldiers.

While Simon Bolivar was expelling Spain from the Northern part of South America, Jose de San Martin was drilling his army of the Andes at Mendoza in Argentina, just across the mountains from Santiago. January 17, 1817, the army, led by San Martin and O'Higgins, started across the Andes to drive the Spaniards out of Chili. Nearly four thousand men, and eleven thousand horses crossed over the summit of the Uspallata pass, 12,500 feet above the sea, 4,000 feet higher than the Great St. Bernard. The conduct of this expedition required more executive ability and foresight than that of Napoleon crossing the Alps.

The two victorious armies neared each other in Peru early in 1822. On July 26, the two great liberators met at the port of Guayaquil and at this conference San Martin agreed to leave the country and give Bolivar free sway.

But of all the liberators of Spanish America, the one who most nearly fills the role of ideal hero is Miguel Hidalgo of Mexico. If he failed anywhere it was in having the executive daring of a great soldier.

In 1752, Don Cristobal Hidalgo y Costilla visited the southern part of the *hacienda*, of which he was governor. One day he stopped for dinner at the farmhouse of Antonio Gallaja, who was one of his tenants. The daughters of Gallaja were famed for their beauty and wit. They did their utmost to gain the admiration of the rich and powerful Hidalgo, but a girl who stood behind their chairs and waited on them attracted his attention most. He found that the little beauty, so coarsely dressed and who was treated by them like a slave, was an orphaned cousin, named Anna Maria.

The following day Don Cristobal returned and asked Anna Maria to take a walk with him. At parting he placed a ring on her finger in token that "My true love hath my heart and I have his."

She was soon Don Cristobal's wife, and, when her second son was born, she little dreamed that he was to be the hero of Mexico and the noblest liberator of all Spanish-America. There was no opening for such aspirations and genius as his but through the Church. His rise was rapid and he might have worn the cardinal's hat if he had been willing to play at politics. But he was a true father of the people. In his resistance to the oppression of the poor, he made bitter enemies and a trial for heresy was instituted against him, but his character was so unassailable and his talents so conspicuous that even in those corrupt ecclesiastical courts only a mild discipline could be secured against him. In time he became *cura* of Dolores with the wider opportunity to ameliorate the conditions and miseries of ignorance and poverty. He revolutionized the district. The house of almost every family of learning became a free school for the poor. He planted vineyards, introduced silkworms, and established potteries, brick kilns, tanneries, and rope factories. He lived with the poor, wore coarse serge cassock, and there was nothing but his scholarly and benevolent countenance to distinguish him from the commonest labourers.

He made extended investigations into literature, philosophy, theology, and jurisprudence, reaching into the mighty domain of liberty of conscience, freedom of thought and hatred of tyranny. Although surrounded by the most ignorant and superstitious people, he formed benevolent and social societies, clubs, guilds, and educational associations. Foreign visitors and the most distinguished men in Mexico began to make Dolores their Mecca. Gradually his influence and eloquence began to turn toward the regeneration of society and the reformation of government. He knew more law than the legal advisers of the king, more theology than the archbishop of the Church, and he could govern better than any appointee that had ever been sent over the ocean from Spain.

Being neither a hypocrite nor a coward, his influence became very offensive to the corrupt minions of church and state. Charges of heresy and sedition were preferred before the Inquisition against the progressive priest of Dolores. He was denounced by those in power as the servant of Satan. He was branded with the awful sacrilege of being a priest who was not an ascetic and who did not believe in flagellation. It was charged that he claimed not to be afraid of the inferno and that he reserved the right of private judgment in the interpretation of the Scriptures. But his life was stainless, and all knew it. He had committed no crime against the law and those who loved him were too numerous to be defied.

In the dilemma someone discovered that he had no right to plant vineyards and mulberry gloves, nor to establish the numerous manufactories through which the community was flourishing. Accordingly he was compelled to stand by with his people and see the best work of years overthrown and his prosperous industries ruined. The vines, trees, and shops were destroyed in one day by the Spanish soldiers, and strict orders were given that they should not be reproduced.

The officials guilty of this deed began to notice with alarm that the Cura of Dolores, though now fifty-eight years of age, was absent a great deal from his parish and province. The humble Creole *curas* of a score of cantons were constantly visiting the little house where Miguel Hidalgo lived. Everybody seemed to know that great secrets were being guarded and there was a hush over affairs that betokened a coming storm.

Unfortunately at this time the Canoness Ittariga fell ill and believed herself about to die. She confided to her confessor, the Cura of Queretaro, that Hidalgo was to head a revolt against the authority of Spain on the first day of November, 1810, and that the Gonzales brothers were acquainted with all the details which were unknown to her. In an hour the Gonzales brothers were called to the governor's house on some alleged business and were secretly arrested and thrown into the dungeon, where there were all of the appliances of the inquisition, to await the speedy arrival of the inquisitor.

The doom of the conspirators for liberty seemed at hand when Doña Josefa Ortiz, the heroic wife of Dominquez, Corregidor of Queretaro, whose house was built against the wall of the prison, heard, while passing to and fro at her work, a series of three sharp taps on the wall from within the prison. Her heart stood still. She understood at once. It was the signal agreed upon with Perez, the jailer. Someone was being held in the inquisitorial dungeon to have the secrets of the conspiracy tortured out of him. In a few minutes trusty messengers were hurried away, one to General Allende at San Miguel, and another to Hidalgo at Dolores, warning them that the plot for liberty was discovered.

The *cura* was in his study, and sitting close around him were a dozen dark-visaged men eagerly listening to his low-spoken words, when a series of raps, betokening a hurried messenger, startled them from their chairs. Hidalgo arose and cautiously asked who was there. It was past midnight and the visitor was clearly one of importance.

"My message is only for the ears of Hidalgo," was the reply.

Hidalgo opened the door. "Speak out, friend," the *cura* said, as the man entered, "I am. Hidalgo and these are as one with him."

The messenger told hurriedly what had occurred and the men turned with blanched faces to the *cura*.

Hidalgo's face lighted up with the animation of one who sees that the supreme hour has come for a great movement.

"Action at once," he exclaimed. "There is no time to be lost. The yoke of our Spanish oppressors shall be broken at once and the fragments scattered over Mexico."

A conference ensued, lasting until daylight, when the street watchman was called in and told to arouse the fifteen workmen employed in the *cura's* pottery, which had been saved from the wreck of industries.

When the astonished men appeared the *cura* told them that the era of liberty had begun and asked them if they were ready to bear arms and devote their lives to its cause.

Weeping with joy they embraced him and the delighted *cura* cried, "Long live our Lady of Guadalupe, and long live our new-born liberty."

It was Sunday morning and the church bell was rung an hour earlier than had ever been done before for mass. The Creoles and Indians flocked from the surrounding country, for it was felt everywhere that something unusual was about to take place. When the people were called together they heard a remarkable discourse. The priest told them that they would not have mass that day, as there was greater need at that time to be delivered from the Spaniard than from the devil.

"My children," he exclaimed, "a new dispensation has come to us this day. Are you ready to receive it? Will you be free? Will you strive to recover from the hated Spaniard the liberty of which you have been robbed for three centuries?"

Great and eager cries arose on all sides and the people pressed around him.

"Today is the day of our salvation," he continued. "We will go to San Miguel for arms. Let all follow me who believe in liberty for themselves and their children."

When General Allende received his message, he hastened to Dolores and soon there was a rabble of four thousand natives, armed with lances, clubs, machetes, slings, and bows. San Miguel was taken and the wild passions of the oppressed people broke forth in such a storm that no man could govern it. The Spaniard had robbed, insulted, and killed for three hundred years without retaliation or punishment, and nothing but brutal destruction could now be expected.

The archbishop excommunicated the priest and all his followers. Every pulpit denounced him as a Lutheran devil. Hidalgo was summoned to appear before the inquisition, and he replied, "I owe nothing to a Spanish inquisition. It is not necessary to be a slave in order to be a true Catholic. I am loyal to my religion, you to your politics."

The religious terrors and the torture of the inquisition were mingled with the dreadful excesses of civil war. The Spaniards fled to the largest cities, women and children were sent to the convents, and all treasures were shipped to foreign countries.

The revolutionists swept everything before them and defeated the army sent out to prevent them entering the City of Mexico. But Hidalgo did not believe his poorly equipped army could take the city. He ordered a retreat to await a more favourable condition. This was a fatal reversal of the victorious advance. It was demoralizing to the natives and encouraging to the Spaniards. In a short time the Benedict Arnold of Mexican liberty appeared. Ignacio Elizondo succeeded in leading Hidalgo into a Spanish ambush at Acatila de Bajen, March 21, 1811, where he was captured. Fearful revenge was taken. The dispirited army was scattered before the invigorated onslaughts of the Spaniards. All the leaders were captured and shot. Hidalgo was reserved for special ecclesiastical degradations. Doña Josefa, the heroine of the revolution, was closely imprisoned for several years, her property confiscated and her children turned out to beggary.

The last words of Hidalgo were, "The knell of Spanish rule in America has been sounded. Liberty for all will come."

He died with the distinction of having been formally sentenced to death by the Pope and the King of Spain. Until the independence of Mexico in 1824, under Iturbide, Hidalgo's head remained on public exhibition in an iron cage, with those of his two generals, as a Spanish warning against all aspirations for liberty. On the cage was this inscription:

These heads of Miguel Hidalgo, Ignacio Allende, and Mariano Jimanez, insidious intriguers and leading chiefs of the revolution, who have seized the property of the Religion of God, and the Real Presence, and shed with the greatest atrocity the blood of faithful priests, and just magistrates; the cause of all the calamities, disgraces, and disasters, which all the inhabitants of this land, an integral part of Spain, suffer and deplore.

Now these relics of patriotism lie in costly sepulchres in the capital, revered by all, and the chief national holiday of Mexico is sacred to the memory of Hidalgo.

Some remarkable characters were brought to the front as dictators in the whirlpool of insurrection and anarchy that followed Spanish-American independence. Rafael Carerra of Guatemala, was typical. He was a half-breed and his youth was spent as a pig driver. Then he became a loafer and gambler, cheating the labourers out of their wages. The turning point in his career as *maranero* and *montero* was brought about by a Frenchman who owned a cochineal plantation. The fastidious gentleman found Carerra behind the wall of the courtyard cheating the gullible French servants out of their money, and so the gambler was promptly kicked off the estate.

Such episodes in his business were not relished and he aspired to robberies on a more extended scale. In the mountains were many thousands of refuges from both justice and injustice. These were chiefly Indian slaves and half-breeds who levied tribute from unfortunate travellers from motives of plunder and revenge. Carerra cast his lot with those people and soon rose to great distinction and influence among them.

Some time previous to this, Morazan had expelled the priests and ordered the destruction of the convents. The robber who had become so influential as to be able to organize the many bands under one head was encouraged to become a revolutionist. Several frightful earthquakes occurred and the priests declared that those shocks were but the beginning evidence of God's displeasure for worse things to follow if the sacrilegious tyrants and usurpers were not driven from Guatemala. A dreadful plague of cholera appeared opportunely and Carerra raised the standard of rebellion. The mountaineers flocked to him from every quarter. After numerous sanguinary engagements where quarter was neither given nor taken, Morazan was driven from the country. In 1843, he tried to raise a counter revolution in Costa Rica, but was captured and shot. Carerra was thus left master of the state with an unassailable support from the half-breeds and Indians.

The Frenchman who had driven the petty gambler from his cochineal plantation, expecting to have his property confiscated by the dictator, and to lose his life for having so summarily treated the con-

THE UNSUCCESSFUL ASSASSIN IN CHAINS ON THE FLOOR OF THE CASTLE DUNGEON.

queror, fled from the country, but was captured by the emissaries of Carerra and brought before the tyrant.

The planter fell on his knees and begged that his family be spared. He expected the dictator to order immediate execution, but to his surprise, Carerra bade him arise, embraced him, and made him treasurer of the state.

Carerra was known as "El Indio" or the Indian, and the aristocracy heartily despised him. At the first opportunity an extended conspiracy was formed against him, but it came to a singular conclusion.

One of the chief officers in the army volunteered to kill him at the grand clerical festival about to take place. The assassin mingled with the throng and pressed nearer and nearer his victim, the conspirators meanwhile closing in around them. Three steps across an open space would bring him to the side of the dictator. The assassin drew his dagger under his cloak, and as he did so the metal-tipped sheath became unloosened and fell to the stone floor with a clinking sound of startling significance. Before he could cover the tell-tale mishap, the scabbard was seen by the President and his friends. The urbane head of the Republic picked the article up from the floor, and with a bow handed it to its owner, who as politely acknowledged the courtesy. The festivities continued as if nothing had occurred to mar the occasion, but an observer, understanding the situation, could have seen a dozen stalwart men of unmistakable Indian type slowly moving nearer the door with the unsuccessful assassin in their midst. Half an hour later he was in chains on the floor of the castle dungeon.

The investigation that followed showed that two brothers of the highest Catalonian family were at the head of the conspiracy. Every device of persuasion and torture was used to make them reveal their accomplices, but they were stoically silent. The officer who had attempted the assassination was condemned to be shot at ten o'clock in the morning, the two brothers to share this fate immediately after.

Every resource of influence and wealth was brought to bear upon Carerra in favour of the two brothers, but in vain. At the fatal hour a volley of shots, heard inside the castle dungeon, signified plainly that the officer had met his punishment. Presently the guards came to the prison with a priest and the brothers were implored once more to reveal the names of their accomplices, but they heroically refused to speak. The elder brother was then led away. A volley of musketry followed and the guard returned with the priest to the younger brother. In vain he was advised to reveal the conspirators. He was then hurried away to a spot where there were two new-made graves and one not yet filled.

"For the last time," said the executioner, "you are asked to reveal the truth."

The boy's lips closed tighter and there was only silence. The firing orders were given, "one, two, three,—." At that instant Carerra sprang forward, snatched the cloak from the condemned man's head, unbound him, and after embracing him, said, "Go join your brother at your home. Guatemala cannot spare such brave sons."

This was one of the singular tyrants that flourished on the soil of Spanish-America. Revolution at last drove him out of power, but he set a strange gauge for New World chivalry.

One of the most romantic episodes told of his methods of justice, occurred near the close of his career. Diego Cortace, a wealthy young Spaniard, holding a large estate in Guatemala, had been so diplomatic that through all the revolutions he had remained unmolested.

In Cobra there was a Creole girl who kept a small store of confections and fruit. She was wise as she was beautiful and none of her numerous suitors knew whom she favoured until her tireless efforts to obtain the release of a Spanish youth, who had been imprisoned for engaging in an insurrection against Carerra, revealed where her chief interest lay. Several visits had been made by her to the dictator in her lover's behalf, but the sentence of death was pronounced and the day of execution drew near, when Maria suddenly disappeared. An Indian from the farm of Cortace came to Carerra and told him that a young woman was being held unwillingly a prisoner on his master's farm.

A score of cavalrymen were at once sent to bring the woman and man before the dictator. A few hours later they returned with the Spaniard and the girl, when she frankly told Carerra that she had gone with some men who came to her with the proposal to break into the castle dungeon and liberate her lover. Instead of going to the castle, the leader, who was Diego Cortace in disguise, seized her and carried her into the country to his house as a prisoner, where he was about to kill her or make her his slave when the rescue came.

Carerra called in a priest.

"The prisoner desires to marry this girl," said he, "and I have concluded that he shall do so."

There could be no protestations against the well-known iron will of the dictator and the marriage was done.

After congratulating the terrified bride, he ordered the prisoner to be taken away. Within half an hour a man returned and gave a signed document to the dictator. A few minutes later the priest came in with the prisoner of the castle dungeon.

"Was this your lover before your late marriage?" asked Carerra of the girl.

She could only bow her head.

"Then let me congratulate you," continued the dictator. "Your husband is dead, you are invested with his estates, and it is my will that you marry your heart's choice, who is now a free man. Priest, perform your duty."

LEONAUR

ALSO FROM LEONAUR
AVAILABLE IN SOFTCOVER OR HARDCOVER WITH DUST JACKET

IRON TIMES WITH THE GUARDS *by An O. E. (G. P. A. Fildes)*—The Experiences of an Officer of the Coldstream Guards on the Western Front During the First World War.

THE GREAT WAR IN THE MIDDLE EAST: 1 *by W. T. Massey*—The Desert Campaigns & How Jerusalem Was Won---two classic accounts in one volume.

THE GREAT WAR IN THE MIDDLE EAST: 2 *by W. T. Massey*—Allenby's Final Triumph.

SMITH-DORRIEN *by Horace Smith-Dorrien*—Isandlwhana to the Great War.

1914 *by Sir John French*—The Early Campaigns of the Great War by the British Commander.

GRENADIER *by E. R. M. Fryer*—The Recollections of an Officer of the Grenadier Guards throughout the Great War on the Western Front.

BATTLE, CAPTURE & ESCAPE *by George Pearson*—The Experiences of a Canadian Light Infantryman During the Great War.

DIGGERS AT WAR *by R. Hugh Knyvett & G. P. Cuttriss*—"Over There" With the Australians by R. Hugh Knyvett and Over the Top With the Third Australian Division by G. P. Cuttriss. Accounts of Australians During the Great War in the Middle East, at Gallipoli and on the Western Front.

HEAVY FIGHTING BEFORE US *by George Brenton Laurie*—The Letters of an Officer of the Royal Irish Rifles on the Western Front During the Great War.

THE CAMELIERS *by Oliver Hogue*—A Classic Account of the Australians of the Imperial Camel Corps During the First World War in the Middle East.

RED DUST *by Donald Black*—A Classic Account of Australian Light Horsemen in Palestine During the First World War.

THE LEAN, BROWN MEN *by Angus Buchanan*—Experiences in East Africa During the Great War with the 25th Royal Fusiliers—the Legion of Frontiersmen.

THE NIGERIAN REGIMENT IN EAST AFRICA *by W. D. Downes*—On Campaign During the Great War 1916-1918.

THE 'DIE-HARDS' IN SIBERIA *by John Ward*—With the Middlesex Regiment Against the Bolsheviks 1918-19.

LEONAUR

ALSO FROM LEONAUR
AVAILABLE IN SOFTCOVER OR HARDCOVER WITH DUST JACKET

THE ART OF WAR *by Antoine Henri Jomini*—Strategy & Tactics From the Age of Horse & Musket

THE MILITARY RELIGIOUS ORDERS OF THE MIDDLE AGES *by F. C. Woodhouse*—The Knights Templar, Hospitaller and Others.

THE BENGAL NATIVE ARMY *by F. G. Cardew*—An Invaluable Reference Resource.

THE 7TH (QUEEN'S OWN) HUSSARS: Volume 4—1688-1914 *by C. R. B. Barrett*—Uniforms, Equipment, Weapons, Traditions, the Services of Notable Officers and Men & the Appendices to All Volumes—Volume 4: 1688-1914.

THE SWORD OF THE CROWN *by Eric W. Sheppard*—A History of the British Army to 1914.

THE 7TH (QUEEN'S OWN) HUSSARS: Volume 3—1818-1914 *by C. R. B. Barrett*—On Campaign During the Canadian Rebellion, the Indian Mutiny, the Sudan, Matabeleland, Mashonaland and the Boer War Volume 3: 1818-1914.

THE CAMPAIGN OF WATERLOO *by Antoine Henri Jomini*—A Political & Military History from the French perspective.

THE AUXILIA OF THE ROMAN IMPERIAL ARMY *by G. L. Cheeseman*.

CAVALRY IN THE FRANCO-PRUSSIAN WAR *by Jean Jacques Théophile Bonie & Otto August Johannes Kaehler*—Actions of French Cavalry 1870 by Jean Jacques Théophile Bonie and Cavalry at Vionville & Mars-la-Tour by Otto August Johannes Kaehler.

NAPOLEON'S MEN AND METHODS *by Alexander L. Kielland*—The Rise and Fall of the Emperor and His Men Who Fought by His Side.

THE WOMAN IN BATTLE *by Loreta Janeta Velazquez*—Soldier, Spy and Secret Service Agent for the Confederancy During the American Civil War.

THE MILITARY SYSTEM OF THE ROMANS *by Albert Harkness*.

THE BATTLE OF ORISKANY 1777 *by Ellis H. Roberts*—The Conflict for the Mowhawk Valley During the American War of Independenc.

PERSONAL RECOLLECTIONS OF JOAN OF ARC *by Mark Twain*.